Creating Contagious Commitment

The Tipping Point is a brilliant computer model of change initiatives as they unfold in large, complex organizations. Change agents need to be informal, keenly aware of the different needs of different types of people, and committed to their purpose. This book shows what to do and what happens along the way, both in the model and in real life.

— Art Kleiner, author, *Who Really Matters* and
The Age of Heretics

Finally, Shapiro breaks through years of psycho-babble and change-speak with practical, grounded steps to gain employee acceptance of change. Much like bringing Doppler weather radar to the ancient Greeks, her model immediately dispels the silly HR superstitions so many leaders worship.

— George Smart, MBA, CEO, Strategic Development, Inc.

Innovative methods used for introducing the concepts of organizational change to employees are both fun and creative. What really stands out with this book is its accessibility; its direct applications to the world of work; and its practical strategies for effectively managing organizational change.

— M. Shields, Ph.D., School of Business,
Christchurch College of Education, New Zealand

This book is a starting point for anyone involved with leading or driving a business change. Once you have a sense of the levers that are key to spreading change, you will be ready to consider your business change in a far more realistic light.

— Roger J. Bushnell, Business Performance Specialist

At last! A book that gives us a concise overview of organizational change management plus a practical approach for action. How many times have we heard about projects that fail because of inadequate change management? Finally, a practical, cost-effective solution via the Tipping Point simulation. Bravo!

> – Helen Sims, Vice President, InfoSENTRY Services, Inc.

Few authors get down to the nitty-gritty business of how to do change right. Andrea Shapiro takes managers, change agents and would-be-champions right down to where the rubber meets the road. She shows that success is no accident and that all of us can drive change more effectively.

> – Carol Willett, VP, Applied Knowledge Group, Inc.

For the first time, it is feasible for the majority of change initiatives to succeed! … An articulate and accessible approach to the Tipping Point model and to uncover the levers of change in your organization.

> – Tim Dempsey, President, TimDempseyConsulting

CREATING CONTAGIOUS COMMITMENT

Applying the Tipping Point to Organizational Change

2nd edition

**Tipping Point Workshops available
in the UK and Europe through:**

Time For Change (Development) Ltd

www.time-for-change.co.uk

* we can facilitate TP workshops for you
* we also run facilitator training so you can
run them for your colleagues or clients

Andrea Shapiro, Ph.D.

CREATING CONTAGIOUS COMMITMENT

Applying the Tipping Point to Organizational Change

2nd edition

Foreword by **Patricia Zigarmi, Ed.D.**
Founder, **The Ken Blanchard Companies**

Published by
Strategy Perspective
Hillsborough, North Carolina
www.4-perspective.com
ccc@4-perspective.com

ISBN: 978-0-9741028-1-8

Library of Congress Control Number: 2009908349

BUS103000
BUSINESS & ECONOMICS/Organizational Development

For Don and Jeanette

Contents

Foreword

It's an honor to write a foreword to the new edition of *Creating Contagious Commitment*. We have found Andrea's thinking and Tipping Point model to be extremely compatible with our work on Leading People Through Change at The Ken Blanchard Companies. There are two fundamental constructs in the Tipping Point model: people's attitudes toward change and the levers of change. People's attitudes toward change reflect their concerns with or unanswered questions about an impending change. We believe concerns are predictable and therefore can be surfaced and addressed. Too often, though, leaders of change ignore people's questions. By ignoring questions about the business case or ignoring personal concerns, these change leaders drive those who are neutral toward resistance. In other words, by not creating dialogue, they create resistance or passive-aggressive behavior. People may comply with the requirement to change in the short run, but in the long run, they revert to old behaviors that sabotage the objectives of the change.

Only when leaders create an energizing environment, as Andrea points out, and only when they use high-involvement change strategies and purposefully create opportunities for peer advocacy, do they gain the cooperation of a critical mass of people and create momentum for a proposed change. Andrea Shapiro's gift to the field of change leadership is her wisdom in identifying the investments leaders must evaluate in terms of the outcomes they are seeking. Are the best investments in orchestrating opportunities for advocates to talk about the change with their peers or are the best investments in infrastructure? How critical is effective sponsorship or aligned leadership? When should investments in mass exposure be made to communicate the business case or vision? These choices are critical to the successful implementation of change. The Tipping Point simulation is the vehicle for the conversation about these choices and for developing a deep understanding of how the levers work systemically.

The dialogue created through the use of the Tipping Point simulation and the solid research explained in this book will predictably help people leading change speak with one voice, create a compelling business case and inspiring vision for the change, develop the right infrastructure and collaborative effort and create the best strategies for holding people accountable for making the change. Faced with having to go sideways or backward at times in order to navigate through constant churn, Andrea's work helps all of us who lead change evaluate what the highest payoff actions might be at any phase of the change process. Whenever we use the collective intelligence of the organization and mobilize everyone's energy by involving them in planning for and executing change, we have a much higher probability of developing the organizational adaptability that is required today and the capacity and capability to lead change in the future.

Our experience in leading Tipping Point workshops for the last several years is that the spirited conversation that occurs in the workshops helps leaders explore new strategies for creating contagious commitment to change—strategies that are far more subtle, often less expensive and far more powerful than the one-size-fits-all mass exposure tactics they default to using more often than not. We are delighted when participants in these workshops conclude that modeling the behaviors expected of others or expanding opportunities for involvement and influence often yield a higher return on investment. As a founder of The Ken Blanchard Companies with a life-long passion for situational leadership in a one-on-one context and adaptive leadership in an organizational context, I wholeheartedly encourage you to get some conversations going in your organization about the important concepts in this book.

Dr. Patricia Zigarmi
Founder, The Ken Blanchard Companies
http://www.kenblanchard.com
Co-Author, *Leading at a Higher Level*
and *Who Killed Change?*

Introduction

Some years ago, I asked the manager responsible for implementing ISO 9001 (a change initiative to establish quality management standards) at a high-tech company how the initiative was going. The company had made huge strides in documenting manufacturing processes, but they were bogged down in engineering. His response was, "It's going fine ... except for the people." The idea of a disembodied change, progressing perfectly but without involving the employees who were supposed to modify the way they work, is amusing. Yet strategies that focus on technical and other easily measurable aspects, such as announcement dates, hardware installation, or training schedules, while expecting magic metamorphoses in the people who are asked to use the new hardware and apply the training, are all too common.

The hard and messy fact is that organizations change only when the people in them change. An effort to modify and improve how work gets done in a company is successful only when people in the organization embrace the idea behind it, work in ways that it prescribes, experience the results, and spread their enthusiasm for it to others. If it doesn't spread, it's dead. Yet the life cycle of many organizational changes follows a similar—and all too familiar—

pattern. The business need is identified. To fill it, leaders marshal forces to implement a new initiative to improve the way work gets done. An executive and his[1] team weigh the options and identify the value proposition that the innovation can offer—and the dangers of not implementing it. Next comes delegation. Implementation is often assigned to a vice-president of Human Resources or Information Technology or another area without line responsibility. Then a project plan is developed, including budgets, milestones, and PERT charts. Perhaps people are hired or incentives are laid out or infrastructure is built or purchased. Too often the focus is on a big announcement followed by a internal marketing campaign that attempts to bring everyone on board. Information on the new initiative is disseminated using various media—including generic training, posters, web pages, mass emails, logo mugs, and so on.

Despite the media campaign, or maybe because of it, cynical comments about "program du jour" or "the emperor's new clothes" persist in the hallways. Employees may demonstrate their apathy by nodding in agreement at the need, the plan, and the leaders, but sit firmly on their hands when it is time to take action. The project plan and the media campaign create a great deal of commotion, but time after time this is followed by a big fizzle. Despite the monetary investment, the media campaign, the skill and energy of the implementers, and the promise of competitive advantage, the company fails to realize the intended benefits from the initiative.

This story is repeated in company after company. In a 2006 McKinsey survey (Vinson *et al.*, "Organizing for Successful Change Management") with over 1500 respondents worldwide, 6% characterized their change as "Completely successful" and 32% as "Mostly successful." The authors say that success depends on creating a clear vision and engaging employees at all levels of the organization. A study published in 2008 by IBM Global Systems

(Jørgensen *et al.*, "Making Change Work") reports that 41% of change projects they looked at were successful. Their research finds that success rests on clear sponsorship and engagement of the people expected to change.

In *Leading Change,* John Kotter estimates that 85% of companies fail to achieve needed transformations. He puts the onus for this lack of success on leaders failing to create a vision and an environment that leads people to do things differently. In "Why Do Employees Resist Change?" (published in the *Harvard Business Review*), Paul Strebel reports that 50–80% of change initiatives in Fortune 1000 companies fail. He argues that this stems from employees not recognizing what is driving the initiative and the value it can bring to the business and to themselves. In another *Harvard Business Review* article, Larry Hirschhorn calls the success rate for organizational change "abysmal." He urges leaders to be more holistic in their approach—guiding new initiatives while tapping into and creating employee commitment and making the most of executives' limited time and attention. In *Managing Transitions*, William Bridges attributes the problem to failure to recognize that people need time to go through the psychological steps of giving up old ways before embracing new ones.

In an essay in *Leading at a Higher Level,* Patricia Zigarmi and her colleagues at The Ken Blanchard Companies articulate a list of predictable reasons that change projects fail. These include failing to surface employees' concerns about the project and the future it will bring, and leaders confusing announcing a change with implementing it. Zigarmi and her colleagues articulate several strategies to address these concerns. Their central strategy is to expand employee involvement and influence. There is more on the Blanchard model in Appendix 1: "More on Models of Change" starting on page 159.

The high-tech firm described in the first paragraph was never able to extend their ISO 9001 success from manufacturing into their engineering departments. They invested in ISO process templates, hired auditors, and put a massive internal marketing campaign in place. Everyone was expected to attend the same half-day course, independent of their job or how ISO was going to affect it. Graduates of the half-day course received ISO 9001 decorated mouse pads and coffee mugs—still available at local garage sales. Few engineers or their direct managers saw the value of documented processes to themselves or to the quality of their product; some saw it as a threat to their creativity. Although the firm did achieve ISO certification, the success from it was short-lived. Without understanding or appreciating ISO, people documented processes but didn't feel a need to follow them. Ultimately ISO was reduced to a dreaded annual audit ritual. This undermined the company's previous success in manufacturing, because engineering processes inevitably affect manufacturing. The documented processes were in place, but without the corresponding change in people's attitudes, the ISO certification ultimately added little or no value to the company.

The Tipping Point Model of Change

The core of this book is the Tipping Point model of change. Rooted in organizational theory and real-world practice and captured in an interactive computer simulation, it is designed to illustrate how organizations implement new and better ways of working to achieve real results. The Tipping Point model goes beyond traditional models in two powerful and unique ways: by leveraging lessons from public health and by applying systems thinking.

The Tipping Point model frames organizational change in terms of the spread of ideas. It is about engendering a word-of-mouth epidemic—a positive epidemic of innovation and improvement in how the company does business. It brings out the importance of Advocates, who are people who not only accept and apply a change but who also demonstrate its value to others in the organization. It delineates the role that leadership plays in building a supportive environment by ensuring that everyone understands the case for change, modeling desired behaviors, and making sure that rewards and infrastructure are aligned with moving in the new direction. It shows how to use commitment from Advocates who are supported by leadership to take the necessary steps to leverage business opportunities.

System thinking enables the Tipping Point model to capture the essential dynamics of change. Systems thinking provides a well-defined language to think holistically, making it possible to go beyond the limits of trying to understand real-world problems by studying their components separately. It provides tools to step back and see the big picture, and overcome the fragmentation of thinking linearly. It captures the complex underlying structure of real-world systems by emphasizing interconnections and feedback loops. Systems thinking can help reveal why there are often delays between cause and effect. It also demonstrates the futility of seeking a single silver bullet to address any problem.

There are two fundamental constructs in the Tipping Point model: people's attitudes toward a change at a given time and levers of change. People's attitudes toward an organizational change effort reflect the value that they recognize in the change plus the support they see for it from their managers. A clear-cut, compelling effort with unambiguous support from management engages people. Levers of change are actions that leaders can take to engage people and help them gain confidence and enthusiasm for a new initiative. No single lever is a panacea. In fact, some should only be used with extreme caution. The real impact of the levers comes from how they *interact* with each other. All the levers need to be addressed or considered in the context of the corporate culture and the nature of the change initiative. No prescription works for every initiative or for every organization. The Tipping Point model provides a framework to make better decisions about how and when to use the levers that can then be applied to different organizations and different improvement efforts.

The Tipping Point model has been captured in a computer simulation that brings it to life. Using the simulation in a structured workshop setting helps people see how the levers of change interact. It sparks new ideas about implementation and potential side effects of actions and decisions. According to Tony Sighe, who has delivered the workshop numerous times, and whose work to assess its effectiveness is described on page 99, "It works because the simulation creates a fun and competitive environment to encourage a full understanding of the levers."

The simulation is not a decision-making or forecasting tool that gives the "right" answer. Rather it is more of an interactive illustration; combinations of tactics that are more likely to succeed in real changes give better results on the simulation. Experimenting with various strategies on the simulation in teams provides a focus for dialogue, for asking the right questions, and thinking deeply about deploying change. When used by teams to create a shared view, it leads to better, more robust implementation strategies for change initiatives. (See "A Focus for Dialogue Enhances Learning" on the following page.)

A Focus for Dialogue Enhances Learning

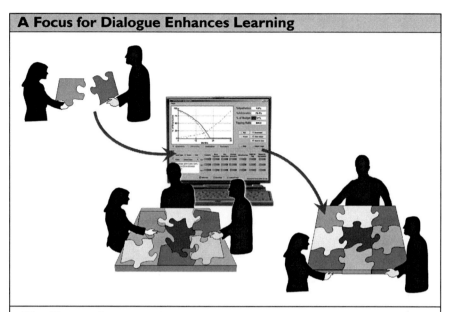

The Tipping Point simulation is not an answer machine or a forecast tool. Rather it sparks dialogue and discussion in a low-risk workshop environment. Team members use the simulation to experience the interactions inherent in change. They try out implementation strategies in an atmosphere of friendly competition.

In workshops, team members often vigorously debate their strategies and discuss trade-offs and costs. Participants have been known to spontaneously stand up to cheer as their strategy unfolds in the simulation. Through this atmosphere of friendly competition, team members learn from each other and gain a shared view of change implementation.

The following account is from a digital wireless equipment manufacturing company that used the Tipping Point workshop when implementing a customer relationship management (CRM) system.[2] CRM entails methodologies and technologies to store and organize information about customers. This information makes it easier to build relationships with customers and to identify their needs. The firm implemented this CRM system during a very turbulent time. Due to market forces, it was reevaluating its product line. As a result of the reevaluation, the firm dropped two mature products that had been bread-and-butter sources of revenue in favor of newer products that had much greater potential for growth. The new products were more complex, integrating several digital wireless services. The firm was developing new devices for the market, which included new networked hardware and software, at the same time that it was implementing a new CRM system for its internal needs.

The Tipping Point Simulation in a CRM Implementation

A rapidly expanding digital wireless equipment firm with five locations across North America was growing beyond its ability to give its customers the care they needed and expected. The firm had no databases for lead generation; rather, all salespeople tracked their own prospects. There was no way to leverage the information known to individual members of the sales force and use it to generate strategies for turning leads into customers or accurately forecast sales. An even bigger problem was the lack of connection between the sales force and what was happening at the other end of the process—in customer service. The firm could not tell if particular customers were having persistent problems that needed to be addressed or if a single problem was surfacing across several customers. Without a tracking mechanism, each problem appeared unique. This lack of information presented a problem for customer service and for sales, both of which could have used the information to better serve the customer. The firm decided to address this problem with a CRM system. The new CRM system would integrate their sales and customer service, enabling them to present a consistent, informed face to their customers.

As a high-tech firm at the leading edge of digital wireless, it is not surprising that they thought of the CRM implementation as a computer network and database project. Initially, they were very focused on the so-called hard-side areas—especially the CRM technology. However, the project sponsor recognized that the implementation team needed to broaden their idea of the CRM implementation—to realize that they were embarking on a large effort that impacted their employees. She had to make it clear that the best CRM system was successful only to the extent that employees fully embraced it and exploited its capabilities.

The Tipping Point simulation helped give them the perspective on the CRM implementation that they needed. Representatives of customer service and sales, together with the project sponsor and the project manager, participated in a workshop that used the computer simulation. As teams vied with each other to create a better strategy to run on the simulation, they began a dialogue that included the people side of implementing CRM. They developed new ideas about implementing organizational change, which they shared as a team. They realized that their plan put too much emphasis on the technology. In the days that followed the workshop, they modified their implementation plan. Through the course of the implementation they used the new language and the common mental models gained from the Tipping Point workshop to keep them on track and to help them ask the right questions when they encountered problems.

It would be wonderful to report that this firm implemented their CRM system 100% on time and within budget. Actually, they were several months late but fairly close to budget. But by bringing the system online—with both sales and customer service data in one place and in use to improve their customer relations—this firm has joined an elite group. Their CRM system is part of the 15–50% of organizational change initiatives that end in success.

I want to help you join this elite group—to successfully implement your organizational change initiatives by making them both contagious and sustainable. Whether your initiative is to improve quality, establish a business model that is environmentally responsible, or understand your customer better, this book provides a framework. It is general enough to be applied to many initiatives and many organizations and specific enough for action planning. You will find both theory and application examples throughout the book. Examples of applying the Tipping Point workshop are set off from the text as in the CRM example above. In addition, there are diagram boxes that summarize the topics covered, which can be used to review the material. When you are done you will be ready to apply the Tipping Point model to your business.

Chapters 1 and 2 of this book provide background on change and organizational theory, public health concepts, and systems thinking. These two chapters also present the basic ideas behind the Tipping Point model, including examples and anecdotes that illustrate real-life applications of the Tipping Point workshop to a range of initiatives.[2] Chapters 3 and 4 develop the model in more detail and give several first-person narratives of its application by leaders in the public and private sectors. Chapter 5 focuses on putting the Tipping Point to work to improve change implementation. It includes an in-depth case study in which the computer simulation is leveraged in a quality initiative at a major corporation. The chapter ends with a checklist to help you assess your organization's readiness for a change initiative.

Some people want to thoroughly understand the motivating theory, and others want to delve immediately into the model and learn by applying it. The book is designed to help you do either. To understand the foundations, continue reading from here. To go immediately to the model, either skip directly to Chapter 3: "Making Change Contagious" or simply review the diagram boxes in Chapters 1 and 2 to get a sense of what the chapters cover. You can go back to read Chapters 1 and 2 after you have a better understanding of the model, or even after you have applied it to your own business and experienced the results.

Chapter 1

Spreading Good Ideas

If the rate of change outside your organization is greater than the
rate of change inside your organization, the end is in sight.
—Jack Welch

Organizations can only institute a change program when employees who are involved in the program understand and have confidence in its value. Building this understanding and confidence is key to effective leadership. By using the Tipping Point model to make decisions and take actions, leaders can motivate employees to accept and adopt a change. To explain its strength, this chapter outlines the influences on the Tipping Point model from lessons learned in public health, systems thinking, and more traditional approaches. It also gives examples of leveraging the Tipping Point model in diverse change initiatives in a range of industries and non-profits.

Organizational Change Is about People

> Those who have changed the universe have never done it by
> changing officials, but always by inspiring the people.
> —Napoleon Bonaparte

Organizational change is a planned effort to improve a business's capacity to get work done and better serve its market. It would be nice to make capacity or quality improvements simply by modifying organizational charts, developing processes, or adding new technologies. Although organizational change might include technology, processes, and organizational charts, it is more than any of these—alone or in concert. It is fundamentally about a change in people. Real change happens when people realize that a new methodology, process, or technology makes them more productive, more efficient, or better able to serve the customers' needs. This realization helps them evolve their attitudes and beliefs about how work gets done.

The seed of any change is an idea about increasing an organization's capacity by improving how work gets done. Experience shows that ideas can be contagious, but they don't simply spread by themselves. Making good ideas contagious requires an environment that nurtures their acceptance. Without such an environment even the best idea about improving work is likely to be met with apathy and indifference.

Apathy undermines and limits the potential of initiatives to provide value, despite any business need they might fill. Consider, for example, the dilution of total quality management (TQM). It went from a rigorous statistical methodology to reduce variation and increase quality in manufacturing to a catch-all that includes everything from customer orientation to people management. Similarly, proponents of business process reengineering (BPR) estimate that 50–70% of BPR efforts fail. Enterprise resource planning programs (such as SAP or Oracle) have had mixed results, despite recognition of the need that they promise to fill (to manage the supply chain and resources). It is estimated that 55% of customer relationship management (CRM) programs fail, despite the importance of maintaining and sharing customer data within a company.[3]

Successful change implementation combines decisions that are centered around what are often called "hard" and "soft" areas. The so-called hard areas include project planning, implementing software, and installing new computer networks. The soft side—the people side—involves the decisions and actions designed to help employees embrace new methodology, technology, and ways of working. The effects of hard-side decisions are easily observed, measured, and adjusted. Because is easier to measure and assess the hard side, it is common for it to get more attention. Soft-side effects tend to be subtler and harder to observe—making them more difficult to measure and evaluate. Yet attention to the people side of change is at least as important as attention to project planning or new technology. According to research by Hans Henrik Jørgensen and his colleagues at IBM Global Systems, the people side is the most important and the biggest challenge to change implementation.[4]

For example, a change initiative could fail because a computer network is not installed properly. However, even if the network is installed perfectly, but employees do not use the new process or the tool supported by the network, then the initiative will fail. Further, fixing a problem with a new computer network is generally straightforward. However, fixing people's attitude that the latest change is a "flavor of the month" and will soon go away is not so straightforward. Thus, attention to the people side of change is often the difference between success and failure.

Unless it becomes part of the way people do their work, there is no business gain from even the best and most appropriate organizational change. Many things—both hard and soft—must coalesce to implement a change successfully in an organization. The Tipping Point model focuses on the area of greatest leverage—the people side. It describes how leadership can cultivate an environment that encourages people in the organization to adopt a change. The model looks at the parts played by those who advocate, those who ignore, those who consider, and those who resist change, and how each can make a difference to whether employees feel committed to seeing it through to success or just waiting it out.

Dan Siems is an experienced Tipping Point workshop facilitator. The following account is based on his experience with a process improvement change effort at a manufacturing firm and illustrates the people side of change. Dan was Chief Improvement Officer at Meggitt PLC, a large publicly held conglomerate primarily serving the aerospace market. Endevco Corporation is an independent business unit within Meggitt that makes extreme environment sensors used in automotive, military, aerospace, medical, and industrial applications. Dan worked with Endevco to help them align their operations with Meggitt's vision for the future. Dan's experience makes clear how people's attitudes toward a change are pivotal to its successful implementation, and how leadership can affect those attitudes. Here Dan describes the background and need for the process improvement and the emotions that it engendered. In Chapter 3, after further description of the Tipping Point model, there will be more of Dan's account of leveraging the model at Endevco.

 Process Improvement on the Factory Floor

To advance their corporate mission, Meggitt directed Endevco to reduce inventories and release cash. Endevco could free working capital by reducing finished goods, work in progress, and raw material inventories, but many stakeholders feared that too little inventory would hurt throughput and customer service levels. To succeed, Endevco had to determine the appropriate inventory levels and hit them. The Sales and Marketing team felt inventories were too low—they could sell what was made. The Operations group—Manufacturing and Procurement—were unsure, but they enjoyed having high inventories as a buffer against perceived fickle customer demand and unstable suppliers. Up to this point in time, the factory Planning team had reacted to inventory levels using experience and deep knowledge of the operation. Using this approach meant expediting was common—sometimes to the point where work didn't move unless it was expedited!

Emotions and stakes were high. Several millions of dollars of working capital could become available if inventories were reduced, satisfying Meggitt's directive to release more cash. However, if inventories were cut too much, resulting in lost sales, many more millions of dollars in long-term lost revenues could result, ruining the business. The group tasked with reducing inventories— Operations—was determined not to disappoint any stakeholders. Tired of "flash in the pan" changes, they wanted an effective, lasting, controlled change in how inventories were managed.

Factory Physics principles and disciplines—understanding the relationship between cycle time, inventory, throughput and variation—were identified as providing the insight needed to determine inventory levels. After collecting and analyzing manufacturing operations and customer-demand data using Factory Physics models and concepts, it became clear that inventories were too high and that there was opportunity to reduce them. Manufacturing cycle time variation was excessive—eliminating this variation would allow further cuts in inventory. Surprisingly, customer demand was stable and predictable and could not account for the high inventories or cycle time variation. Evidently, the perception that customer demand was unstable had contributed to inflated inventories.

Through the Factory Physics analysis, the VP of Operations realized that several changes needed to be implemented before inventories could be reduced, specifically: 1) Manufacturing needed to reduce cycle times (and cycle time variation). This required training and effort from his team. 2) Sales and Marketing needed to commit to a manufacturing plan based on knowledge of demand data and trends. This could end expediting, but it required believing the historical (and very stable) customer demand data. 3) Planning needed to stop relying entirely on expe-rience and deep knowledge of the operation and instead use the data from the new systems to plan and run the factory. This meant they had to believe the new system and stop overriding it. The planners worked for the Purchasing group (outside the VP's sphere of control) but were key to changing internal factory dynamics. 4) Management support was needed to "buy time" from corporate. It would take time to implement these changes and for results to become evident.

—Dan Siems

The VP of Operations made the end state clear. To successfully implement Factory Physics when the emotions and stakes are so high, it is essential to get the four constituencies on board and in full support. This is not unique. People's mindset can impede or facilitate change and often make the difference between success and failure. The Tipping Point addresses how new ideas spread by looking at people's attitudes toward them and how to affect those attitudes. In Chapter 3: "Making Change Contagious," Dan finishes recounting his experience to show how the Tipping Point workshop was used at Endevco to implement this process improvement program.

Lessons from Public Health

To illustrate how lessons learned from public health apply to implementing changes within an organization, think about how the flu spreads. The key to flu spreading is contact; it spreads when people who are contagious with the flu come in contact with well people. Some of the well people—depending on a variety of interacting factors, such as the status of their immune system, how much sleep they get, the transmissibility of the flu strain, local sanitation facilities, etc.—begin incubating the disease. After a period of time, some incubating people may become contagious and able to spread it to others. Some incubators—depending on various interacting factors—never become contagious. They just return to the pool of well people.

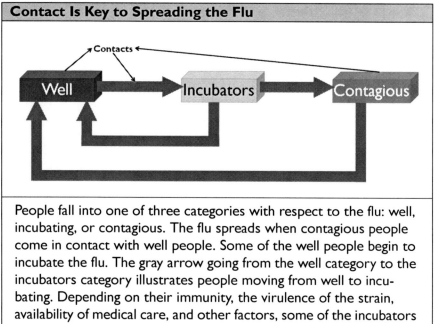

Contact Is Key to Spreading the Flu

People fall into one of three categories with respect to the flu: well, incubating, or contagious. The flu spreads when contagious people come in contact with well people. Some of the well people begin to incubate the flu. The gray arrow going from the well category to the incubators category illustrates people moving from well to incubating. Depending on their immunity, the virulence of the strain, availability of medical care, and other factors, some of the incubators will become contagious themselves and thus able to spread the flu. Others will just return to the well pool. After the flu runs its course, contagious people will also return to the well pool, as illustrated by the gray arrow from the contagious category to the well category.[5]

The familiar pattern of the flu spreading also applies to organizational change, but the goal is to turn the pattern inside out—to use it to spread ideas about new and better ways of working and create a *positive* epidemic. Ideas spread when people with expertise, experience, and enthusiasm advocate them. These Advocates are "infected" with a new way of doing work. When people have this enthusiasm, they talk to others. They talk to people who are apathetic toward the idea. Perhaps they haven't heard about it yet or they believe the change will be like the 50–85% of previous initiatives which failed or were abandoned before full implementation.

When Advocates contact Apathetics, one of two things can happen. Some of the Apathetics begin to think about it; they mentally test it against their own beliefs and experience. They begin to incubate the idea. Other Apathetics will just ignore it. They may nod in agreement, but they take no action and remain Apathetics. Depending on many factors such as whether or not leaders set an example, whether there are adequate tools, or the reward system is aligned to the change, some Incubators may, with time and experience, become Advocates themselves. Other Incubators will fail to see the value and become Apathetics again. If supported, Advocates will remain Advocates, and continue to spread their enthusiasm for the idea. Others will decide that the organization is not really serious about the change and return to the Apathetics pool, or even leave the company. See "Organizational Analogy—A Positive Epidemic" on the following page.

Applying the model of a contagion and associated concepts from public health to social questions has a long history. In his 1962 book, *Diffusion of Innovations*, Everett Rogers applied this model to large social changes, such as family planning, the adoption of medicines, and disease prevention. He also recognized the work of earlier researchers in the area such as Gabriel Tarde in the early part of the twentieth century, as well as Bryce Ryan and Neal C. Gross (a 1940s study of Iowa farmers' acceptance of new seed corn).[6] In the 1970s, Thomas Schelling, the 2005 Nobel Laureate in Economics, applied the contagion model to numerous situations such as people crossing a busy street in groups large enough to feel safe, attendance at seminars, and the so-called white flight to the suburbs. Schelling also coined the term "tipping point" to describe situations where small increases in numbers reaches a critical level and causes a system-wide effect. In a 2000 bestseller,

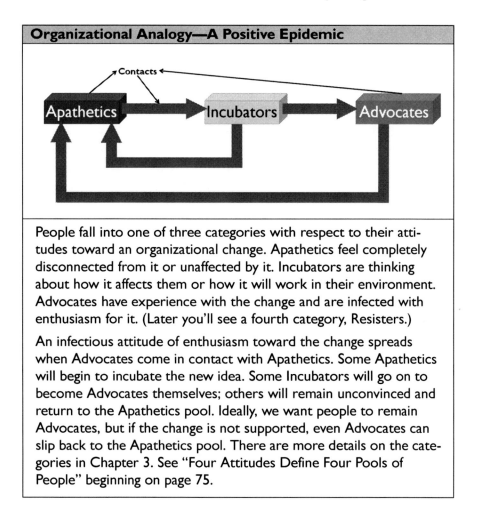

Organizational Analogy—A Positive Epidemic

People fall into one of three categories with respect to their attitudes toward an organizational change. Apathetics feel completely disconnected from it or unaffected by it. Incubators are thinking about how it affects them or how it will work in their environment. Advocates have experience with the change and are infected with enthusiasm for it. (Later you'll see a fourth category, Resisters.)

An infectious attitude of enthusiasm toward the change spreads when Advocates come in contact with Apathetics. Some Apathetics will begin to incubate the new idea. Some Incubators will go on to become Advocates themselves; others will remain unconvinced and return to the Apathetics pool. Ideally, we want people to remain Advocates, but if the change is not supported, even Advocates can slip back to the Apathetics pool. There are more details on the categories in Chapter 3. See "Four Attitudes Define Four Pools of People" beginning on page 75.

The Tipping Point, Malcolm Gladwell looked at the common characteristics of disease and social epidemics. More recently, John Sterman examined the dynamics of a word-of-mouth epidemic in the marketing of new products.[7]

Making use of the contagion model in organizational change to improve implementation results is an important advance. Building the model into an interactive computer simulation makes its lessons real and helps demonstrate how change happens and how to foster its spread. The model also illustrates the many interacting factors that affect the spread of change.

Interacting Factors

One important lesson from public health is that you cannot consider a disease in isolation from the environment in which it is happening or the people whom it affects. Diseases that originated in Europe provide an example of how the same pathogen spreads differently in different populations. By the era of New World exploration, measles and smallpox were no longer widespread plagues in Europe. However, after contact with Europeans, these same diseases wiped out the inhabitants of entire Native American villages. Native Americans had never been exposed to these diseases, and thus did not have the immunity that Europeans had developed over generations. Cholera provides an example of how the environment affects how a disease spreads. Cholera spreads quickly in areas without clean water supplies, but it is virtually unknown where water is clean. These are just two examples of the same pathogen having a different effect in a different population or in a different environment.

The spread of ideas—even good ideas—works analogously. Numerous interacting factors affect how far and how fast an idea circulates. One set of circumstances can foster the spread of a good idea while a different set can kill it. The speed and distance with which an idea or an organizational change spreads depends on its innate value, the amount of contact between its Advocates and the people who are Apathetic to it, and environmental factors such as leaders who lead by example, rewards and recognition for successful implementation, and infrastructure investments that support the change.

In *The Tipping Point*, Malcolm Gladwell examines three categories of factors that make the difference between changes that spread rapidly and become social epidemics and those that stagnate and eventually die out. To describe these three factors, he coined the terms *content*, *carriers*, and *context*. In the case of the flu, these correspond respectively to the flu strain itself, the people with the flu, and the environment in which the flu is (or is not) spreading.

A standing ovation provides a familiar example that illustrates the interplay of content, context, and carriers in social change. Think back to the last concert or play you attended. Perhaps it ended with a standing ovation for the performers. Whether or not the whole audience stands to applaud depends on more than just the quality of the performance. First consider content; standing applause spreads differently than quiet, polite clapping and still differently from booing or throwing tomatoes. Carriers have a clear role. Enthusiastic applause from front-row audience members that everyone can see is more likely to spread than similar clapping from people standing up in the rear. Context is also important. The venue, whether it is a huge outdoor arena or a small community playhouse, affects the likelihood of people standing up to applaud. Content, context, and carriers also interact. For example, front-row carriers with the same level of enthusiasm will have a different effect in a auditorium than in an outdoor concert.

Although Gladwell does not specifically consider organizational changes, they are nonetheless examples of social changes; they involve the spread of an idea through the interaction of the idea itself, the people, and the environment. It is worth looking more deeply at content, carriers, and context from an organizational change perspective.

Compelling Content refers to a change that will bring value to the company and motivate employees. In a 2009 *McKinsey Quarterly* article, Carolyn Arken and Scott Keller describe what makes a change compelling: a holistic explanation that appeals to employees' interest in their contribution to society, to their customers and shareholders, to the people they work with, and to themselves. Thus, compelling content includes both the potential to increase the company's ability to serve customer needs (by improving the way work gets done) and employees' belief that the change is worth working toward.

Carriers are those who are infected with the idea; they are the Advocates described previously. Not all carriers are equal. Starting with the *Appropriate Advocates*—people who have the respect of many others—will help an idea spread more quickly. Appropriate Advocates are not simply cheerleaders for the change but colleagues who have expertise in the area being changed and experience with the change itself. They are Advocates because they understand the gap the change is expected to fill, and they see how the change will fill it.

Context is the environment where the change is being implemented. It consists of the support—or all too often the lack of it—that management provides for the change. The importance of this support should never be underestimated. Few, if any, changes have succeeded without an *Energized Environment* of infrastructure, incentives, and leadership aligned with the change.

Good leaders make the content compelling to employees by ensuring that everyone understands the reasons behind the change. They create the energized environment that is aligned with the change, and foster the appropriate Advocates to spread the change. In *A Simpler Way*, Margaret Wheatley and Myron Kellner-Rogers advise leaders to adjust the way that they think about their responsibilities. They say that a leader's role is to create a clear vision, then make sure that connections, information, and resources are available and aligned, and let the organizing processes work.

The organizing processes work through making the content compelling, energizing the environment through leadership, infrastructure and rewards, and finding and leveraging appropriate

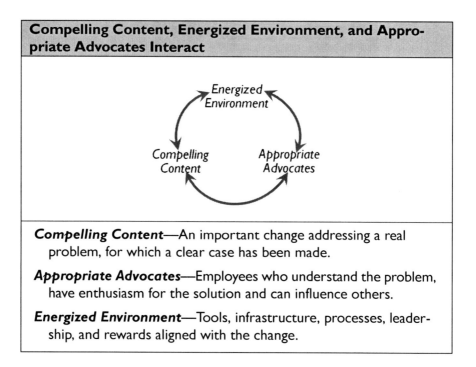

Compelling Content, Energized Environment, and Appropriate Advocates Interact

Compelling Content—An important change addressing a real problem, for which a clear case has been made.

Appropriate Advocates—Employees who understand the problem, have enthusiasm for the solution and can influence others.

Energized Environment—Tools, infrastructure, processes, leadership, and rewards aligned with the change.

Advocates. Failing to live up to potential is often a result of not making a compelling case for change, falling short of energizing the environment, or neglecting to identify the Advocates of the change and provide them the support they need. The following account of failing to make a Knowledge Management system compelling and not aligning it with an energized environment is adapted from the experience of a company that we will call Medical Machines.

Knowledge Management at Medical Machines

Medical Machines had been very successful in producing automated bench-top diagnostic tools for hospitals. Their innovative medical test devices had significantly increased the diagnostic capability of smaller hospitals, offering their customers both cost savings and an increase in the types of patients that these hospitals could serve. As a result, Medical Machines enjoyed significant market share.

A new start-up company entered the market with smaller, more portable, and more automated equipment, initially designed for home nursing care and physicians' offices. These devices used wireless transmission to increase their capabilities by connecting to major hospitals when necessary. The start-up got Medical Machines' attention when they began marketing their devices to small hospitals, thereby winning over some of Medical Machines' customers. To compete, Medical Machines started to develop smaller, wireless devices. The sales force lacked familiarity with the new devices, and there was poor communication between sales and engineering, As a result, Medical Machines began having problems meeting promises made to customers. They felt that a knowledge management (KM) system would help engineers and sales personnel communicate better on new projects and existing engineering change orders. This would allow them to leverage the learnings about each product and from each sale and thus avoid making promises that they could not keep.

Although a KM system requires networks and software, it is fundamentally a cultural change. Employees must view the value of their own knowledge differently. To succeed, there must be incentives for employees to share knowledge. If both engineers and salespeople do not see the value to themselves and to Medical Machines of sharing information, then even a technically perfect KM system will fail. Medical Machines assigned the KM implementation task to the vice-president of information technology. From a technical viewpoint, he was the person best able to implement a KM system. His team immediately began the process of adapting a commercially available system. However, no research was carried out to understand what aspects of the corporate culture were limiting knowledge sharing. Furthermore, no members of his team were targets of the change, so they lacked an appreciation of how it would be used.

Within one year, the system was made available to both engineering and sales, complete with logo mugs and a huge fanfare on the value expected. However, nothing was done to foster knowledge sharing. There had been rewards for implementing the KM software, but no rewards or recognition for sharing knowledge. Few employees saw a value to themselves of sharing knowledge. In fact, some resisted using the KM system because they felt that sharing knowledge might give away their edge to receiving bonuses and promotions or might even undermine their position within the corporation. There were also no metrics in place to measure the value of sharing knowledge to Medical Machines as a whole, and without data the case could not be shown for the value to the company as a whole. The KM system became a little-used and expensive piece of software.

At Medical Machines, the people who were expected to use the KM system did not understand its value. Far from enthusiasm for a new tool that could make them more productive, they felt threatened by it and thus resisted using it. Seeing the value and feeling supported are prerequisites to a willingness to take the risk to do things differently.

Medical Machines made a very common error: they mistook the content of the change for the change itself. They saw it as a technology implementation and did not recognize the cultural changes that were needed to make it successful. As a result, they failed to identify Advocates of knowledge sharing, so they were hardly in a position to support them and help them spread their knowledge and enthusiasm. Furthermore, no one took the time and effort to listen to the employees' concerns, which could have easily been addressed by making the business case clear and by initiating incentives for sharing knowledge. In short, Medical Machines did not create an environment for change, rather they created an environment of apathy and resistance to change.

I once heard Russell Ackoff, a leader in applying systems thinking to business challenges, tell a story about a CEO who failed to recognize the importance of the environment and of Advocates in implementing change. In a meeting with all his general managers, the CEO compared the efficiency of all the processes that were common to all the facilities within the company. He noticed that no single plant was more efficient than the others in all the processes. Shipping may have been more efficient in one plant relative to other plants, whereas in another plant billing was better than in all of its sister plants.

This CEO decided that for each common process he would pick the most efficient one, from whichever plant it originated, and implement it across all the plants. The CEO was warned that he was taking a very non-systemic view of the processes. His plan did not take into account the effect of the environment on a process, the many points of interaction between a process and the rest of the plant that contributed to its efficiency — or inefficiency. The plan also did not account for the specialized skills of those people doing (or interacting with) each process in each plant.

Nevertheless, the CEO went ahead with the plan. Millions of dollars and a great deal of effort later, the result was that all the processes in all the plants were less efficient than before. The CEO didn't see that a process was efficient in one plant partly because of its interactions with other processes inside the plant, partly because of the people who executed it, and partly because of the environment outside the plant.

Ackoff's example does not imply that a practice can never be reused in a different environment. Rather, it implies that successful reuse demands first knowing why the practice works, how its environment influences it, and how it influences its environment. Successful reuse also requires fully understanding any special skills and enthusiasm that people bring to their job. Only after all these sorts of similarities and differences are understood can reuse bring value.

Resistance

There is another analogy from public health that is useful in understanding organizational change — resistance. People can develop resistance to a disease and sometimes complete immunity to it. Resistance is a factor that can affect the implementation of an organizational change as well. Incubators may fail to see the value of a change or believe that it is inappropriate to the organization or feel it threatens their own position, and so they begin to resist the change. This gives a fourth pool of people in the organization — Resisters. Together, the four pools — Apathetics, Incubators, Resisters, and Advocates — form the *attitude pools* used by the Tipping Point model.

A certain amount of resistance is inevitable, and some resistance can be useful. Resistance to change can come in several forms. The first consists of legitimate, constructive concerns about a change. For example, the change could be incomplete, too much of a cultural jump for the organization, or not understood by those expected to implement it or inappropriate or ill-timed.

Resistance that stems from constructive concern should be thought of as an early warning system. A great deal can be learned from Resisters with genuine concerns that can strengthen a change and avoid failure. Such resistance can spark exploration to find better methods of implementation or improvements to the change itself. When constructive concerns are aired and addressed, they become a source of innovation and enhance the likelihood of success. However, if the corporate culture interprets legitimate concern as a challenge to the change or to management's authority, then an opportunity to learn and improve is lost. Worse, it will probably cause the Resister to become more covert in his resistance — thus having more potential to undermine the change initiative.

A marketing director at a large telecommunications company told me that she sees it as her *responsibility* to question every organizational change touching her department. Occasionally, this tactic backfires on her, and she is labeled a troublemaker. However, her experience has shown that when she is consistent and constructive with her questions, the result is usually positive. Addressing problems early on saves the company time and money, often with a positive effect on her own department and budget, and it yields a stronger change initiative.

Not all resistance is constructive. A more dangerous source of resistance comes from too much exposure to changes that were supposed to be important improvements but ended up as nothing more than big announcements followed by slogans on coffee mugs. Resistance resulting from overexposure to change initiatives that were not fully implemented, despite their potential, can be very damaging. When employees have seen changes over-hyped in the past they begin to associate needed changes with meaningless hype. Even worse, changes are sometimes misrepresented, such as claiming benefits for employees that in fact are nonexistent. Either case creates an atmosphere of cynicism about change. The potential to create cynicism underscores the importance of only undertaking organizational changes that are important, presenting them honestly, and being prepared to fully sponsor them through to successful implementation.

A third form of resistance comes from fear. It could be fear of the uncertainty of acquiring new skills or adapting to new processes. It could be fear that the change will result in people losing jobs, authority, influence, or bonuses. These possibilities make people feel that the future is outside of their control. It is the stuff of rumors and unrest. The reality is that, depending on the change, these things are a possibility; some people may lose their influence or even their jobs. Candor and honesty is the only way to approach this source of resistance. If a merger or reengineering effort will result in a lay-off, spell out the reasons and the numbers as clearly as they are known. Otherwise, you can be sure that the rumor mill will portray them as many times worse. Reliable and accurate information is one way to slow the flow of rumor. Knowing the real picture and believing in its accuracy gives people a sense of control and has the potential to alleviate some resistance.

Sources of Resistance
Concern with the change or its applicability
Overexposure to hyped and unsupported changes in the past
Fear of the unknown and of loss

Besides coming from different sources, resistance can manifest itself overtly or covertly. Overt resistance can be a source of valuable information if it is presented constructively and listened to. Covert resistance sabotages a change. In *Managing at the Speed of Change*, Daryl Conner recommends developing a culture that encourages employees to be open when they have questions about change. He even suggests developing a course on how to resist change, where people learn how to present their concerns constructively. The flip side is that there must be safety from reprisals for raising concerns, and people must feel that management will consider the issues that they raise and act on them appropriately.

It is easy to see the role of trust in addressing potential resistance. Trust takes many forms. People need to trust that it is safe to air their concerns. This means being able to trust that a change that they put effort into is real and not just hype, and that they have been told both the upside and the downside of a change. Honesty and trustworthiness of the sponsor and leaders of the change are vital. In their popular book, *The Leadership Challenge*, James Kouzes and Barry Posner report that their years of research demonstrate that honesty is the single most consistently valued leadership characteristic. Trustworthiness may not eliminate resistance, but untrustworthiness will definitely increase it, as illustrated in the following account of a quality initiative in a call center.

Misrepresenting a Quality Improvement Initiative

A large call center that operated under contract to another firm embarked on a quality initiative. The targets of the quality initiative were the customer service representatives (CSRs) who answered the calls. The call center wanted to ensure quality, as measured by metrics defined by the contracting firm. The quality initiative was presented to the CSR team as a training initiative whose goal was to raise the performance of every CSR.

All the supervisors received literature that they were to share with their people. This literature indicated that there would be increased call monitoring to identify areas where training could improve overall customer service and thus improve the quality metrics. This literature further claimed, very specifically, that the call center leadership was not trying to weed out "bad apples." However, their real intention was to improve quality by monitoring employees to find those who were responsible for any problems and reprimand or replace them.

It did not take long for the CSRs to realize that they were being lied to as they were written up for minor quality problems that had been ignored previously. Employees became cynical about the company's true commitment to improve quality through focused training. They did not feel safe enough to raise their concerns to management, but they raised them at the water cooler. When the training did not materialize, many began covert resistance by doing the absolute minimum of customer service. Morale dropped seriously, affecting even the most competent CSRs, with a corresponding drop in quality. The call center lost two of its best CSRs and experienced its first serious threat to contract renewal in ten years.

The lesson from the call center is that this change failed because it was not approached honestly. Improving quality was a good idea and CSRs recognized it, so the content was compelling. The CSRs were ready; they wanted to improve quality. The change would have been more likely to succeed (or perhaps been modified for success), if the CSRs had been told honestly about its nature. Instead the environment created by the call center contractor was toxic, and they lost the very employees that they wanted to retain. Worse, it soured the remaining employees for future change. The story of the call center is not uncommon. Most change efforts are either abandoned before implementation or are implemented and fail to live up to their financial potential.[8]

Supporting Change

> It does not require a majority to prevail, but rather an irate,
> tireless minority keen to set brush fires in people's minds.
> —Samuel Adams

When people *do* recognize the value of an organizational change to their own productivity and work environment, they become energized by it and alter their way of working. With experience they become Advocates of the change. If the environment is conducive and the Advocates are respected for their contribution to the organization, then their enthusiasm becomes contagious. Advocates can spread the word about the effectiveness of an initiative and how it improves their achievement in their own jobs. As Advocates spread the word, others may begin to consider the value of the change to their own job effectiveness. When others alter the way they think about their jobs and become committed to the change, it can spread through the organization like a positive epidemic.

The Tipping Point draws on the fact that change is a process and that the targets of change have a key role in its success. In *The Human Side of the Enterprise*, Douglas McGregor puts forth Theory Y to describe the behavior of individuals at work. He argues that when employees are committed to objectives, they seek responsibility and demonstrate imagination and creativity. The way to gain commitment is to be sure that people understand the purpose of an action. When they do, they exercise self-direction, often coming up with better methods and doing better work. The Tipping Point builds on Theory Y. It recognizes that the people who are the targets of a change are typically the best people to explain a change and its value to a colleague—especially when they know that the change is well supported by management.

The path of a change initiative is rarely (if ever) smooth and straight. Change initiatives can expose hidden problems or create flux or make the situation worse before it gets better. In *New Rules for the New Economy,* Kevin Kelly describes this very succinctly by saying, "Don't confuse a clear view for a short distance." A clear vision of the end state is important, but it doesn't imply that the road to it is clear or straight. (See "The Path to Change is Rarely Straight or Smooth" on the following page.) This underlines the importance of Advocates who are affected by the change. They are closer to the action than are the sponsors of the change. They are in a position to navigate the small dips, bumps, and plateaus between now and the end state. They can explain to others affected by the change specifically what to expect along the way. They can listen to concerns and convey them to the change leaders when appropriate.

The Tipping Point leverages the power of existing Advocates. However, regardless of how important a change may be—no matter how enthusiastic its Advocates may be initially—the idea will *not* spread throughout the organization without leadership support. In *Harvard Management Update,* David Sirota and his colleagues report the results of their survey research on maintaining employee enthusiasm and motivation. Their research shows that providing a clear, concise explanation of purpose and recognizing achievement can be motivators. More importantly, failing to do so is a demotivator. Managers who are expediters and who ensure that employees have what they need to get their work done create and maintain enthusiasm. These managers also

The Path to Change is Rarely Straight or Smooth

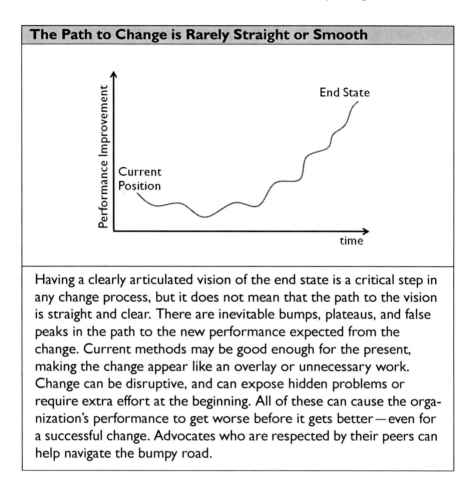

Having a clearly articulated vision of the end state is a critical step in any change process, but it does not mean that the path to the vision is straight and clear. There are inevitable bumps, plateaus, and false peaks in the path to the new performance expected from the change. Current methods may be good enough for the present, making the change appear like an overlay or unnecessary work. Change can be disruptive, and can expose hidden problems or require extra effort at the beginning. All of these can cause the organization's performance to get worse before it gets better — even for a successful change. Advocates who are respected by their peers can help navigate the bumpy road.

emphasize the importance of two-way communication, and they seek out employee involvement and feedback. They foster an environment where people begin to think differently about their work and where Advocates of change can have a greater influence.

To lead an organization from its current position to the goal state, there are two types of support that managers can provide: People Support and Environmental Support. People Support consists of actions that leaders can take that directly affect people's attitude toward a change, such as fostering meetings between Advocates and others or making information about the change available. Environmental Support is about building the sustaining structures and environment for change. It includes making the business case clear to all stakeholders, putting necessary tools and processes in place, and rewarding those who support the change.

If neither type of support is in place, failure is almost guaranteed. All but the most diehard Advocates will recognize the futility of supporting a doomed change and move their energies elsewhere. If either one of People Support or Environmental Support is insufficient, there will be problems, even if the other support system is adequate. If People Support is high but Environmental Support is low, then employees will see the change only as happy talk with no supporting tools or resources, creating cynicism toward it. If Environmental Support is high but People Support is low, employees will be unfamiliar with the change and confused about their roles.

Environmental Support and People Support Interact

Environmental Support		People Support	
		Low	High
High		Confusion slows acceptance. Wasted $$	With support, the Advocates help ensure success.
Low		Lack of support almost guarantees failure. Wasted $$	Cynicism slows acceptance. Wasted $$

Used together, People and Environmental Support foster Advocates' enthusiasm for a change. If People Support is high but Environmental Support is low, then employees' expectations will be raised, but they will lack the tools to make the change. This creates cynicism that tarnishes the current change and future changes. If Environmental Support is high but People Support is low, then tools will be available, but employees will not know what to expect from the tools or how to use them, causing confusion.

Another dangerous way to waste investment is by creating an environment of forced compliance. A "do it or else" threat is not an endorsement of a change, and it does little to engender the kind of commitment that spreads under its own enthusiasm. When a change is supported, people are much more likely to listen to the Advocates of change and take their experience seriously. It is leadership's responsibility to create the climate for commitment: one that helps people understand the organizational change, provides the tools to make the change work, and builds incentives and an atmosphere in which enthusiasm and success can grow.

Recognizing the Limitations of Forced Compliance

I was introducing the concepts behind the Tipping Point to a large and respected government agency. I had barely begun when someone voiced a notion that the more politically astute people in the room may have been thinking, saying, "We don't really need Advocates. We just need compliance." For a moment, I considered reminding the group that they were starting their second try at implementing this particular change. Instead, I reminded them that compliance has never spread like wildfire. True commitment never stems from fear, nor can it be forced. Contagious commitment to an organizational change develops when people understand its value to their own jobs, and they feel supported to make the change.

The group went on to use the Tipping Point computer simulation. It helped them realize how change can spread when people who are committed to it demonstrate and advocate the change to others in the organization. After working with the simulation, participants recognized the leverage that comes from supporting Advocates and encouraging them to share their commitment with others. The woman who thought that they could get by with just compliance became one of the most vocal supporters of the lessons from the Tipping Point model. Months later, the group was still using the Tipping Point language to help assess their progress with the change implementation.

In a *Systems Thinker* article titled "Dancing with Systems," Donella Meadows, a pioneer in systems thinking, said that systems, with all their feedback and interactions, are inherently not controllable. Rather than trying to control the system and the people in it, reinforcing behaviors that you need and encouraging them to develop further is a much stronger approach and more likely to yield results. As no one has an unlimited budget for change, identifying the most effective People and Environmental Support for a specific change in a specific organization is time well spent.

Helping an organization think about the complexity of implementing change in a more holistic way can be a change in itself. The following account is by Helen Nicol, who worked with the National Health Service (NHS), the United Kingdom's publicly funded healthcare provider. The NHS is a large and comprehensive public health service, employing over 1.5 million people. As part of the leadership team for a extensive program with a substantial Information Technology (IT) component, Helen participated in a Tipping Point workshop. She recognized the value of the Tipping Point's methodology as a tool for increasing awareness of the intricacy of managing change and thereby broadening the approach to implementing the IT-enabled program. In the following account, Helen gives some background on the change, the organization, and getting buy-in to use the Tipping Point workshop. In Chapter 4, she completes her story by describing how she leveraged the workshop.

Tipping Point Concepts Applied to an IT-Enabled Program

Having attended a Tipping Point workshop, I felt that there was considerable potential for using it to help people involved in the major IT-enabled change program taking place within the NHS, the National Program for IT. I recognized the value of the Tipping Point workshop as a tool for increasing awareness of the complexity of change management.

I proposed adopting the Tipping Point workshop as a developmental tool for the IT program because the workshop was experiential and encouraged reflection and knowledge sharing, and enabled those with little experience of change management to "get it" quickly, safely and in an engaging way. However, the wheels of bureaucracy move slowly and it took many months to get to the stage of running a pilot with individuals willing to attend the training and become facilitators.

What were my tactics for gaining buy-in? I used elements of the Tipping Point methodology. I used Contacts, tapping into my existing networks to identify those who would be interested and who would have the time and skills to deliver workshops. I organized pre-pilot workshops to gain senior level support for the project. This was an essential step and enabled me to gain buy-in from the organizations taking part.

One of the first workshops of the pilot had a real practical impact on the plans of a project team working on implementing new systems. Reviewing their existing approach in relation to the Tipping Point model led them to completely rethink their communications and engagement activities.

We are now starting to see real value from running the workshops, with many believing the Tipping Point workshop should be mandatory for those taking part in the program of change. There are a number of key Advocates who will deliver the workshop in their own organizations and we hope to increase the number of facilitators who are able to deliver and apply the workshop in their own organizations.

—Helen Nicol

Critical Mass

There is nothing more powerful than an idea whose time has come.
—Victor Hugo

Traditional linear thinking leads to the assumption that cause and effect are proportional: the greater the effort the greater the impact. However, change is not linear. Huge efforts can have frustratingly small effects. For example, large one-size-fits-all training programs can have little—or even negative—impact despite large investments in energy and resources. On the other hand, small efforts like informal networks to support Advocates, can have significant effects.

Nuclear physicists have developed the concept of "critical mass," which refers to the minimum amount of nuclear fissionable material needed to sustain a chain reaction. If a critical mass is not attained, there is no chain reaction (or it is not sustained) and the energy dissipates. With a critical mass, the chain reaction begins at the atomic level, gains incredible energy, and literally explodes beyond control. In *Critical Mass: How One Thing Leads to Another*, Phillip Ball applies similar ideas to many social and political situations. His ideas are rooted in a theory of diffusion developed more than half a century ago.

Using data from a range of studies across several different fields, Everett Rogers developed a general theory of how any innovation diffuses through a population. In *Diffusion of Innovations*, first published in 1962, Rogers describes his finding that the inclination to adopt an innovation is normally distributed; it has the familiar bell-shaped frequency distribution. He classified people along the distribution into five categories, from the most to the least inclined to accept an innovation. The groups were called innovators, early adopters, early majority, late majority, and laggards.

Innovators (about 2.5% of people) want to try something *because* it is new and offers unexplored potential. Early adopters (about 13.5%) are motivated by new ideas and the possibilities they offer, but they tend to be more cautious about their adoption decision than innovators. The early majority (the next 34%) are not interested in innovation for innovation's sake, but they also don't want to be the last to adopt an innovation if they believe it has practical value. The late majority (the next 34%) wait to see that the innovation really works, as evidenced by half the people adopting it before they adopt. Laggards (the final 16%) are the last to adopt an innovation, if they adopt it at all.

Rogers described the process that individuals go through to decide whether or not to adopt an innovation or change. (This process is addressed in greater detail in Appendix 1: "More on Models of Change.") Conceptually, this decision process entails first garnering knowledge of the change, then being sufficiently persuaded that it might work to make a tentative adoption decision. This is followed by informal testing before a confirmed adoption decision is made. Channels of communication and connections between people are major factors, because for each group, the decision-making process is influenced by the experience of the previous adopters.

Early adopters tend to be opinion leaders, because they are well informed about the innovation while simultaneously being more judicious about adopting a new technology or change than the innovators. The early majority plays the essential role of connecting the innovators and early adopters with the late majority, who are slower and more deliberate in adopting an innovation. The innovation begins to become a new standard as more of the early majority adopt it, paving the way for the late majority.

According to Rogers, critical mass is achieved when enough people have adopted an innovation or a new idea to generate momentum and ensure that further adoption is self-sustaining. Communication between adopters and those considering the innovation has a large role in making the adoption self-sustaining. Thus, for a change to spread through an organization, it has to move from the more pioneering early adopters to the early majority. To make this happen Advocates need the skills to communicate and influence others about the change.

Skilled Advocates

Experience with the change is key. It allows Advocates to explain the value of the change in very concrete terms. It allows them to "tell stories" that people can identify with. Regardless of how much experience and enthusiasm an Advocate has, no matter how much she is respected for her expertise, it takes specific skills to help spread good ideas. It is important to grow the pool of Advocates, and it is equally important to develop skills within the Advocates to spread change. Influential Advocates know how to listen to the concerns of Apathetics and Resisters, and to raise important concerns to leaders who can address them.

Warren Scott of Oakwood Learning has facilitated Tipping Point workshops in a number of different firms. He has also done extensive survey research to discover how leaders, managers, and employees from a mixture of disciplines are influenced by others. He has used this research to help Advocates become articulate communicators and good rapport builders. In the account on the following page, Warren describes applying his survey research to how Advocates can influence Apathetics (and even Resisters) to achieve critical mass for a change initiative.

Influencing Skills

Research evidence suggests that at the heart of influence is the sense of being fully attended to. Advocates who do this have the ability to genuinely pay attention to the other person and demonstrate that they are listening. This involves having a focus on the Apathetics' ideas, needs, feelings, and thoughts. Active listening, questioning and summarizing are part (but not all) of the behaviors of attending. The Advocate needs to be open to influence as well as be encouraging and friendly.

In order to be convinced, Apathetics need to realize why change is imperative and understand why the current situation is unsatisfactory. This can be because of current problems, or it can be based on the premise that what we are doing now will not work in the future. People need to understand and feel the dissatisfaction themselves. Then they really will buy into the change. When this element is not in place, the change often gets put to the bottom of the priority list.

People will own the change if they can see a link between their own personal goals, hopes and aspirations, and the goals of the change. The Advocates need to be able to explain not only how the change will benefit the company but also how the change will benefit individuals. People value something that is scarce or special. If they feel that the change is groundbreaking, exciting and new, then they are more likely to feel it is an opportunity.

Effective influencers need to portray their ideas with conviction. They are able to be assertive with their wants and have crystal clarity when outlining them. However, they are never aggressive. As a result of being clear, they are seen as decisive, determined, committed, and resilient. People will follow influencers who are clear about the way forward. We do not need to see every detail of the future, but we need to see enough so we can understand what we are heading toward, and what the future will look, sound, and feel like. Influencers are focused on achievement; they are consistent and persistent in their views. Data, anecdote, evidence, and metaphor bring a change to life. Some people deal well with numerical data, others prefer a metaphor. Using both is a powerful combination. Advocates need to connect emotionally as well as logically with people's decision-making process.

Good influencers are open and share their knowledge, the reasons for their decisions, and their thinking, so they are perceived as honest by others. Being open seems to be a key skill in sharing experiences, knowledge, and information. Influencers who are transparent in their dealings engender trust. They are seen as transcending the petty political struggles of the everyday workplace.

People align with their own clear commitments. Evidence suggests that people are likely to act on the change, if they have said they will to others. People will act consistently with their commitment if we get the commitment to be active (they play a part), public (they tell others) and voluntary (they have a choice).

—Warren Scott

Advocates who are good influencers can help make a change contagious. However, in *Managing at the Speed of Change*, Daryl Conner advises Advocates not to confuse their own enthusiasm for the change with proper sponsorship. Pulling together the organization to support the change can only be done by management. Many academics and practitioners have written about aligning and guiding change. The next section outlines the work of four of them whose ideas influenced the Tipping Point model. There is more detail on their work in Appendix 1: "More on Models of Change," which also contains a description of a model developed by Patricia Zigarmi and her colleagues that leverages the Tipping Point simulation.

Aligning the Organization and Guiding the Change

Kurt Lewin was one of the earliest social scientists to study change in organizations. His research, described in *Field Theory in Social Science,* indicates that change is a process of reducing the forces of the status quo, then transitioning to the new attitudes and norms, and last establishing a stable state with tools and rewards aligned to move forward with the change. Without a compelling case for the change there is little chance of moving the organization from the status quo. The tools, leadership, and rewards aligned with the change are needed to establish the new norms and prepare for a new stable state.

In *Organizational Diagnosis,* Marvin Weisbord introduces a high-level framework to characterize the many interacting factors needed to understand organizations and make changes within them. The framework is called the six-box model for the six categories in it: purpose, structure, relationships, rewards, helpful mechanisms, and leadership. Chapter 3: "Making Change Contagious" develops the levers of change used in the Tipping Point model more fully, all of which are influenced by one or more of Weisbord's boxes. Weisbord deliberately defines the boxes broadly to reflect the many different types of actions that each may represent. A similar approach is taken in the Tipping Point model with the levers of change.

In *Managing Transitions,* William Bridges describes three psychological phases people go through before they can accept a new change: letting go, neutral zone, and new beginning. Bridges warns that it takes time for people to go through these stages. Leaders are usually farther along in the psychological process than their employees because they have known about the change longer. They often mistake employees' being in an earlier phase with a lack of cooperation. The time needed to go through these transition phases, as well as the time for the adoption-decision that Everett Rogers describes (see "Critical Mass" on page 38), accounts for the time spent in the Incubators category before a person can become an Advocate.

The sooner that a change can demonstrate benefit, the easier it is for employees to recognize its value. In his book *Leading Change,* John Kotter outlines eight steps for change leaders. Creating "early wins," such as a successful pilot program, is one of these steps. A significant change can take quite a bit of time to put into operation. An early win can create credibility for the change while full implementation is in progress. Initial accomplishments, which are measured, rewarded, and recognized, help the early majority see the value from the change and become Advocates of it, and they can then influence people in the late majority. Once a change does speak to a broad cross-section it will have gained a critical mass, so that further adoption becomes self-sustaining.

Creating a Model of Change

> Things do not change; we change.
> —Henry David Thoreau

The Tipping Point model is concerned with the underlying structure that drives the events we experience. It connects the outcomes and behaviors of a system to the interconnections, interactions, and feedback of its constituent parts, and illustrates how this behavior evolves through time. The history of the Tipping Point simulation development explains some of its strengths. It was initially derived from existing organizational theory (especially the authors mentioned in the previous section), systems thinking, and public health, but experience was needed to put numbers to the theory and create a computer simulation. I began by interviewing a group of people who had been responsible for implementing a variety of change initiatives. These people had well over seventy-five years of change management know-how among them. I used their expertise to refine the interrelationships in the simulation.

After creating a working prototype of the simulation, I took it on an extensive road show to gain feedback from organizational leaders, graduate students and professors in business schools, and from individuals with experience in organizational change. With this feedback, I modified and improved the Tipping Point simulation several times. The simulation has had input from literally hundreds of change sponsors, change leaders, managers, and people affected by change. This input gives it a great deal of face validity. That is, the variables in the simulation interact in ways that are consistent with the experience of people who are knowledgeable and experienced in implementing change.

A Dialogue Tool, Not an Answer Machine

In a Tipping Point workshop, it is not unusual for people to place too much emphasis on the actual numbers. They seem to be reacting to the Tipping Point simulation as if it were a predictive tool—as if it were saying, "If you put 5% more on this lever, then change will happen 2.5 months earlier." This misses the point completely. The numbers and plots in the Tipping Point simulation are representative. No simulation can provide specific answers for every initiative in every organization. Nonetheless, the dynamics are similar across organizations and changes. The Tipping Point workshop uses the simulation to present these dynamics and promotes experimentation with them.

Questioning the numbers and plots that Tipping Point simulation generates doesn't help people understand how to implement change. However, questioning it on the basis of the *structure* can be the first step in grasping the underlying model and gaining insight from it. The structure that underpins the model, combining four attitudes toward a change and seven change levers and the interactions between them, is relevant to every organization. Questioning the underlying structure sparks serious discussion about change and about how ideas spread. It provides a jumping-off point for adapting the concepts in the Tipping Point model to a given organizational change and getting real value from it.

There is an adage that says, "All of us together are smarter than any one of us alone." By creating implementation strategies in teams, Tipping Point workshop participants develop a shared mental model that combines and develops the knowledge of each team member. A shared mental model fosters future participation and collaboration when it is time to deploy a real change; this then helps teams create more effective deployment strategies that address interactions which otherwise might have fallen through the cracks. The platform for experimentation that fosters dialogue among team members is a significant value-add of the Tipping Point workshop.

Moving Forward

Key Concepts

⟡ At its core, change is about people. Organizations can only change when the people in them change. People's attitudes toward a particular change initiative fall into one of four categories: Advocates, Incubators, Apathetics, or Resisters. Advocates have experience with the initiative and see its potential. Incubators are thinking about it and weighing it against their experience. Apathetics may not know about the initiative, or they may feel disconnected from it. Resisters are actively challenging the change initiative.

⟡ Ideas can be contagious. When ideas are about new and better ways of working, we want to make them contagious. Lessons from public health can show us how to make an organizational change both contagious and sustainable.

⟡ Understanding the power of influencing is an important skill for Advocates to have. It helps them explain their own experience and enthusiasm for the change, but it doesn't take away the leaders' responsibility to create the environment where the value of the change can be easily demonstrated.

Points to Ponder

⟡ Is your change initiative properly supported? Do the sponsors of the initiative really believe that it will make a difference? Can they clearly explain the business case behind the change? Do they do so early and often?

⟡ Do you know who the Advocates of your change are? Is there a plan in place to support them? Is there support in the environment to encourage Incubators to become Advocates?

❥ Do you know where there is resistance to this change and what it stems from? Have you talked with Resisters?

❥ If Resisters have good ideas, are you prepared to act on them?

❥ When you initiate a change are you considering the people who actually have to change the way that they do their work? Are you leveraging their expertise?

Chapter 2

Thinking Systemically

The whole is more than the sum of its parts.
—Aristotle

Standing on shore, the ocean appears flat. Despite globes or transoceanic trips, the impression of flatness is inescapable. In *The Fifth Discipline*, Peter Senge says, "Reality is made of circles, but we see straight lines."[9] Seeing straight lines limits our perception—while at the same time giving the impression that we see it all. Just as looking at the horizon is seeing only part of the Earth, so linear thinking captures only part of the picture. Systems thinking is a discipline that gives us the tools to overcome this limitation. The Tipping Point relies heavily on systems thinking, and this chapter presents some of its basic concepts.

Links and Loops

> Our actions run as causes and return to us as results.
> —Herman Melville

A system is a collection of components that interact together to function as a whole. Systems thinking is a methodology to understand a whole system by recognizing how the components interact. Attention to interactions necessarily leads to attention to time and delays, since interactions evolve over time and are affected by delays. Similarly, attending to interactions leads to concern with closed feedback loops, since interactions are typically not linear. An organization is a social system, and an organizational change is a change to this system. Organizations are also embedded in larger systems—community, national, economic, political, industrial, and global systems. Using systems thinking to understand an organizational change initiative means attending to interconnections of the components of the initiative and how they fit into the rest of the company, accounting for the role of time in implementation, and understanding how feedback affects the initiative and the people implementing it.

Systems Thinking Skills

The bright red cardinal at my bird feeder is a lovely creature and is also a system. The bird is a collection of components—wings, feathers, eyes, ears, and internal organs—that all interact together to form a showy red bird. The cardinal's characteristics, such as his ability to see, fly, and chirp, emerge from the interaction of these components. Each component of the cardinal must be integrated into the whole bird to express its function. His wings cannot fly unless they are part of the cardinal, nor can his eyes see. The reverse is also true. To function as a cardinal, all of its parts must be integrated into a whole. The cardinal—like any system—is not defined by its components alone but by their interactions and interrelationships. Thinking in terms of the whole by recognizing the interconnection of the components to create the whole is a key systems thinking skill.

Thinking in Wholes	
• A system is a collection of components that interact together to form a whole. • Each component must be part of the whole to perform its essential function. • The whole gets its characteristics from the interactions of the components.	• A cardinal is a collection of components—all necessary to the cardinal's existence. • Each component—wings, organs, etc.—has its function only as a part of the whole cardinal. • The cardinal gets its characteristics from interactions of the wings, organs, and other components.

Systems thinking is a disciplined way to think in terms of wholes and to understand the behavior of the whole system in terms of the interactions of the components that make it up. Three skills are key to systems thinking:

• Thinking in wholes, rather than parts.

• Recognizing the role of time in understanding the system's dynamics.

• Understanding the effects of feedback loops.

The interactions between components in a system result in the system behavior—or dynamics. Dynamics unfold over time. At times components interact very quickly, causing the resulting system behavior to appear almost instantaneous. At other times there are delays. One way or the other, time is always a consideration in understanding the behavior of a system. Looking for patterns of behavior over time and recognizing the role that time has in creating these dynamics is another systems thinking skill.

Together the components and their interactions are called the structure of the system. The interactions between components inevitably lead to closed loops called feedback loops. In a feedback loop, the output of a component at one point in time becomes its own input at a later time. The cardinal provides a simple example. What the bird sees is a function of where he has flown, and where he has flown is a function of what he has seen previously.

In sum, the system behavior, which evolves over time, is what we experience from a system. These dynamics result from the interactions of the components in the underlying structure.

The Two Types of Feedback Loops

There are two types of feedback loops—reinforcing and balancing. Together they form the building blocks of systems thinking. Each type of loop has it own characteristic dynamics: reinforcing loops cause growth or decay, and balancing loops give stability. Reinforcing and balancing combine with one another to generate more complex dynamics. The following two sections go into further detail about reinforcing and balancing loops. A couple of examples demonstrate these two types of loops and their application to understanding real-world problems. If you are unfamiliar with the notation used in closed loops, Appendix 2: "Notation of Links and Loops" explains it more thoroughly.

Reinforcing Loops

The screech that we have all heard when the loudspeaker and microphone in a public address system are placed too close is a familiar example of a simple reinforcing loop. It happens when the microphone is placed where it can pick up the loudspeaker's output. The microphone feeds this sound to the amplifier, which amplifies it and sends it back out to the loudspeaker. Then the microphone picks up the sound from the loudspeaker and sends it to the amplifier for further amplification. This cycle of amplification continues very rapidly until the speakers' ability to put out sound is saturated, and everyone's ears hurt.

A business-related example of a reinforcing loop is the interaction between an employee's performance and the support that he gets from management. An employee whose performance goes up tends to get more support in the form of better assignments, bonuses, needed training, and so on. This drives performance up even further. This doesn't imply that management support is the only influence on employee performance. It is just one straightforward influence, and it forms a simple reinforcing loop.

Reinforcing loops can result in either growth or decline. An employee whose performance goes down tends to get less support, and less support causes performance to decline further. The two possible patterns of growth or decline that can come from a reinforcing loop are shown on the following page.

Reinforcing loops never add stability to the system, and they never reach equilibrium. They compound incremental change, either up or down, with more change in the same direction. Whether causing growth or decline, the basic pattern is always the same. It starts off slowly and gains momentum over time (due to the compounding). However, nothing can grow (or decline) forever. So reinforcing loops are always mixed with some limiting factor (perhaps another reinforcing loop competing for the same resources).

A Simple Reinforcing Loop Example

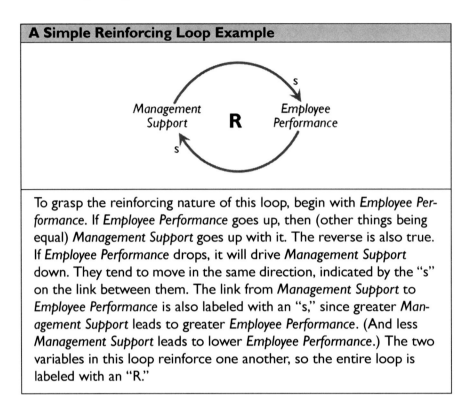

To grasp the reinforcing nature of this loop, begin with *Employee Performance*. If *Employee Performance* goes up, then (other things being equal) *Management Support* goes up with it. The reverse is also true. If *Employee Performance* drops, it will drive *Management Support* down. They tend to move in the same direction, indicated by the "s" on the link between them. The link from *Management Support* to *Employee Performance* is also labeled with an "s," since greater *Management Support* leads to greater *Employee Performance*. (And less *Management Support* leads to lower *Employee Performance*.) The two variables in this loop reinforce one another, so the entire loop is labeled with an "R."

Balancing Loops

Balancing loops are the other building block of systems thinking. Instead of steady growth or decline, balancing loops will approach a goal or steady state. The heating system in your home is a good example of a balancing loop. Working in combination, the thermostat and the furnace are designed to keep the temperature in the house close to the temperature set on the thermostat. When the house temperature drops below the setting, the thermostat senses the difference and turns on the furnace. The furnace will remain on until the thermostat senses that the house temperature has risen above the setting, at which time it shuts off. Since it is colder outside, the house will begin to cool down. When the temperature drops below the thermostat setting, the process starts all over

Behavior over Time from a Reinforcing Loop

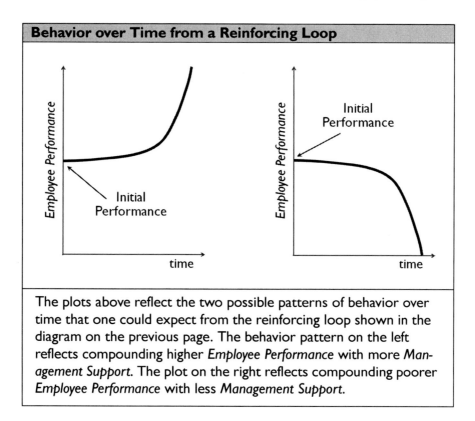

The plots above reflect the two possible patterns of behavior over time that one could expect from the reinforcing loop shown in the diagram on the previous page. The behavior pattern on the left reflects compounding higher *Employee Performance* with more *Management Support*. The plot on the right reflects compounding poorer *Employee Performance* with less *Management Support*.

again. The loop that illustrates this interaction is described in Appendix 2: "Notation of Links and Loops."

Balancing loops with very small (or no) delays approach a steady state (sometimes called their goal state) very smoothly. However, delays are inevitable, and they result in oscillation. In your heating system, it takes time for the furnace to heat the house, and for the thermostat to respond to the change in house temperature. These delays result in temperature oscillation around the thermostat setting. The quicker the thermostat senses the house temperature and the faster the furnace heats the house, the smaller is the oscillation in temperature.

Returning to the employee performance example, a simple balancing loop is also involved. There is an interaction between the employee's performance, the number of assignments that he gets, and the quality of the resulting work. This interaction forms a balancing loop. As performance goes up, the number of assignments tends to go up, since assignments often go to people who do them well. Up to a certain point, the employee can handle the larger workload, but after too many assignments, quality will tend to go down. Quality is a big part of overall employee performance, so the worker's performance will begin to fall. With lower performance he will tend to get fewer assignments. With fewer assignments the employee can spend more time on each one, so quality goes back up, which drives performance up and so on.

A Simple Balancing Loop Example

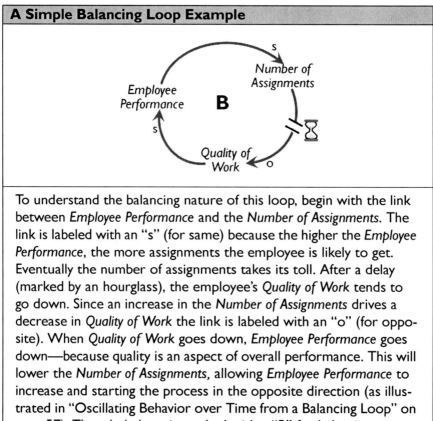

To understand the balancing nature of this loop, begin with the link between *Employee Performance* and the *Number of Assignments*. The link is labeled with an "s" (for same) because the higher the *Employee Performance*, the more assignments the employee is likely to get. Eventually the number of assignments takes its toll. After a delay (marked by an hourglass), the employee's *Quality of Work* tends to go down. Since an increase in the *Number of Assignments* drives a decrease in *Quality of Work* the link is labeled with an "o" (for opposite). When *Quality of Work* goes down, *Employee Performance* goes down—because quality is an aspect of overall performance. This will lower the *Number of Assignments*, allowing *Employee Performance* to increase and starting the process in the opposite direction (as illustrated in "Oscillating Behavior over Time from a Balancing Loop" on page 57). The whole loop is marked with a "B" for balancing.

However, during the time it takes to recognize that the employee's performance has gone down, the number of assignments continues to rise. This rise drives the quality (and thus performance) further down than it would have otherwise. This lower quality causes the number of assignments to be reduced more than necessary to reach an optimum number of assignments (and its incumbent equilibrium performance). The employee now has fewer than the optimum number of assignments, so his quality and performance rises. This leads to more assignments, and eventually more than he can handle, causing a drop in performance. The delay between the reduction in the number of assignments and the increase in quality of work causes oscillation around the equilibrium performance.

Oscillating Behavior over Time from a Balancing Loop

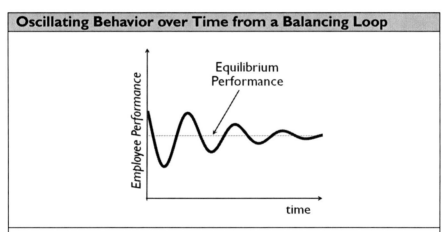

This graph of *Employee Performance* over time is typical of a balancing loop with delays. It begins at an initial performance, which could be above or below the equilibrium. For illustration, assume it starts above. Employee performance will drop below the equilibrium because it takes time for the increased number of assignments to affect quality and thus performance. This drop in performance causes the number of assignments to drop and quality to increase. As quality increases, performance overshoots the equilibrium because it takes time to build up quality and performance. The overall behavior of the system over time is to oscillate around the equilibrium performance. The oscillation will dampen as the number of assignments gets closer to the number the employee can handle.

In the employee performance balancing loop, the longer it takes for the quality to go down (or be recognized as going down) the greater the amplitude of the oscillation. Conversely, the quicker the reduced quality is noticed, the lower the oscillation. Hopefully, the employee's manager learns the relationship between number of assignments and quality of work and adjusts the employee's workload to close to the optimum number of assignments. If so, this will tend to dampen the oscillation over time.

Combining Reinforcing and Balancing Loops

Reinforcing and balancing loops combine to describe any system. The events that we experience result from the components of reinforcing and balancing loops interacting with one another. To see this, return to the employee performance example. Both the balancing and reinforcing loops already described have an effect on employee performance, and they can be combined to give a fuller description. The reinforcing loop will contribute continuous increase or decline in performance, while the balancing loop will push performance toward a stable equilibrium. Both of the two loops simultaneously affect employee performance. The interaction of the loops will better describe the system behavior than either one alone.

Initially, the reinforcing loop would dominate and cause a steady increase (or decrease) in performance. But, nothing can grow (or decline) forever, and there is a limit on employee performance. Eventually the effects of the balancing loop would begin to dominate, causing oscillation around an equilibrium.

These simple link-and-loop diagrams illustrate the potential of thinking in terms of the interrelationship of the components that make up a whole system. They provide a language to understand the interactions and delays to give a fuller picture of the mecha-

Combining a Reinforcing and Balancing Loop

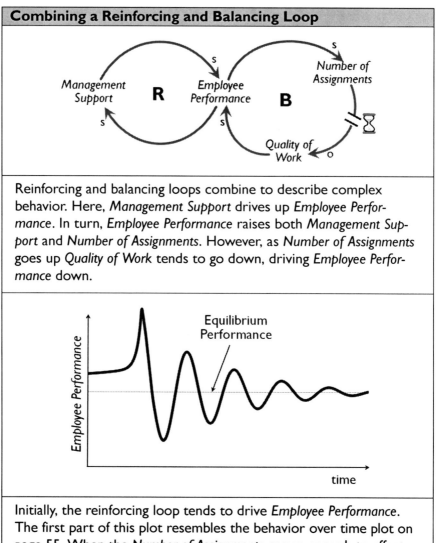

Reinforcing and balancing loops combine to describe complex behavior. Here, *Management Support* drives up *Employee Performance*. In turn, *Employee Performance* raises both *Management Support* and *Number of Assignments*. However, as *Number of Assignments* goes up *Quality of Work* tends to go down, driving *Employee Performance* down.

Initially, the reinforcing loop tends to drive *Employee Performance*. The first part of this plot resembles the behavior over time plot on page 55. When the *Number of Assignments* grows enough to affect the employee's *Quality of Work*, then the balancing loop begins to dominate—driving *Employee Performance* toward its equilibrium. Due to the delay (in recognizing lowered performance and reducing assignments), performance tends to fall below the equilibrium. The *Number of Assignments* is then reduced, and the performance exceeds the equilibrium, bringing on more assignments which reduce performance. Eventually *Employee Performance* oscillates around the equilibrium, yielding behavior over time that resembles the example illustrated on page 57.

nisms driving everyday events. Given the complexity of organizations, becoming skilled at creating and reading link-and-loop diagrams provides transparency that can lead to finding areas of leverage to address problems and improve outcomes.

The Power of Two

> I think there is a world market for maybe five computers.
> —Thomas Watson, Chairman, IBM, 1949

It is easy to be trapped in linear thinking and underestimate the growth caused by a reinforcing loop. One example of thinking linearly about change is attempting to affect one person at a time through the organization. Another linear idea is expecting huge efforts like company-wide awareness trainings to have a large effect on people's attitude toward a change or vice versa. Realizing that an idea can be contagious—as in the Tipping Point—changes this way of thinking. Suppose one person is "infected" with commitment for a change that is important for an organization's future. Her enthusiasm is catchy and she spreads it to two people, each with contagious commitment to the idea. Both of them spread it to two more people each, giving four new people with the same infectious commitment. With every step the number of new people infected with the idea doubles.

Doubling is a simple example of exponential growth, and a thought experiment can illustrate its power. Imagine a chessboard. On the first square, mentally place a single grain of sand. On the second square, place two; on the third place four grains. Continue doubling the number of grains in each square until all of the 64 squares on the chessboard have been filled. How many grains of sand would be on the chessboard? Most people guess around

100,000 or sometimes as high as a million or two. The number of grains of sand is actually 18,446,744,073,709,551,615—or more than 18.4 quintillion![10] It is hard to imagine a number this big, let alone wonder how many miles of beach it would take to collect 18.4 quintillion grains of sand.

Even more interesting than this enormous number is the fact that when half of the squares (that is 32 squares or 4 rows) have been filled, there are slightly less than 4.3 billion grains of sand on the chessboard. When half the chess squares are filled, only about two ten-billionths of the total grains of sand would have been placed on the board. This pattern of slow rate of increase at the beginning followed by an explosive increase later is characteristic of exponential growth. The transition between slow and explosive growth is called "the tipping point."

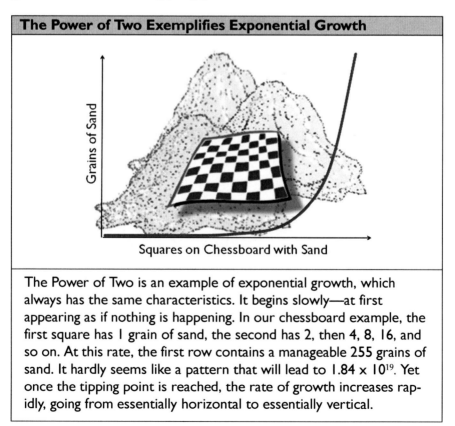

The Power of Two Exemplifies Exponential Growth

Grains of Sand

Squares on Chessboard with Sand

The Power of Two is an example of exponential growth, which always has the same characteristics. It begins slowly—at first appearing as if nothing is happening. In our chessboard example, the first square has 1 grain of sand, the second has 2, then 4, 8, 16, and so on. At this rate, the first row contains a manageable 255 grains of sand. It hardly seems like a pattern that will lead to 1.84×10^{19}. Yet once the tipping point is reached, the rate of growth increases rapidly, going from essentially horizontal to essentially vertical.

Other examples of exponential growth include bacteria multiplying in a favorable culture or compound interest in a savings account (which is described in more detail in Appendix 2: "Notation of Links and Loops"). In these examples, the increase with each step is not necessarily doubling. In a savings account, it is quite a bit less than doubling; the interest rate is usually small, but the result is still exponential growth. It has the same characteristic growth pattern: starting out small and hard to notice, but after reaching its tipping point, increasing very rapidly.

Acceptance of the Internet and email is another example of exponential growth. Initially, few people outside the Department of Defense and defense contractors had even heard of email. Later universities were included; eventually businesses and individuals were brought online. There is a simple reinforcing loop driving the expansive growth of the Internet. As more information was put on the Internet, more people wanted to be connected, increasing demand for new hosts. More hosts went online, allowing more information and newer content to go on the Internet, so even more people wanted to be connected and so on. Thus the Internet fueled its own growth. As more information and functionality was put on the Internet, it became more valuable to its users, so more people wanted to be connected. The demand was so high that the growth of Internet hosts reached a tipping point, that is, a time before which the growth is slow and after which it becomes very rapid. Once the tipping point was reached, the Internet grew beyond the imagination of the original developers. This engine of growth is summarized in "A Reinforcing Loop Captures Internet Growth" on the following page.

If a new idea or concept is in an environment where it becomes contagious, it can reach its tipping point. Only after the tipping point is reached is there rapid acceptance. Epidemics—whether the disease or the word-of-mouth variety—express this characteristic exponential growth rather than linear growth. The idea or

A Reinforcing Loop Captures Internet Growth

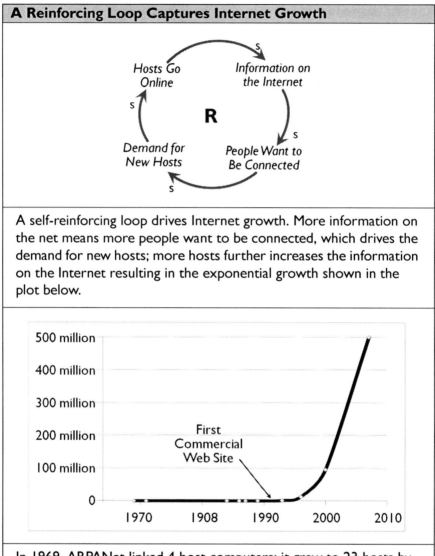

A self-reinforcing loop drives Internet growth. More information on the net means more people want to be connected, which drives the demand for new hosts; more hosts further increases the information on the Internet resulting in the exponential growth shown in the plot below.

In 1969, ARPANet linked 4 host computers; it grew to 23 hosts by 1971 and over 1000 by 1984. In 1986, with National Science Foundation involvement, the number of hosts went from 5000 to 28,000. 1987 brought the first commercial Internet provider; by 1989 there were over 150,000 hosts. In 1991, the World Wide Web made it easier to create and access content, yielding over 1 million hosts by 1992 and the first commercial web site in 1993. Web browsers' availability in 1994 facilitated e-commerce. In 1996 there were 12.9 million hosts; this soared to 93 million by 2000 and surpassed half a billion by early 2007.[11]

innovation or change appears to be going nowhere at first, but if it reaches its tipping point, it suddenly takes off. See "How Fast an Idea Is Spreading: The Tipping Ratio" starting on page 96 for a measure of whether or not a tipping point can be reached.

When implementing change, the goal is to harness the energy of exponential growth—to recognize when it is happening and nurture it. Because it starts off small and gives the impression that nothing is happening, it can be very discouraging. Yet not everything that starts off small expands exponentially. Know what is causing the small growth; if there is no self-reinforcing loop then there is no possibility for exponential expansion. Investigate what you can do to create a self-reinforcing engine of growth supporting the change. There is more on this in "Levers of Change in Action" beginning on page 106. If it is a self-reinforcing loop causing exponential growth, be patient and encourage it, especially if it is in the early stages.

System Archetypes

> Never doubt that a small group of thoughtful, committed citizens
> can change the world. Indeed, it's the only thing that ever has.
> —Margaret Mead

Through years of observation systems thinkers have noticed many patterns that repeat themselves in different contexts. They refer to these repeating patterns—and the structure that gives rise to them—as system archetypes. For an example, think back to the time before DVD and certainly well before Blu-ray, when there were two competing videotape recording formats: Betamax (or Beta) and VHS. For a while it was not clear which format would become the standard for home recording. Eventually Beta became a memory, and the home recording market was dominated by

VHS. Few experts claimed that VHS was a superior product technically; in fact many professionals continued to use Beta. How did VHS come to be synonymous with home video recording? The "success to the successful" system archetype can help us see how.

In the success to the successful archetype, two competitors seek a limited resource. In the Beta versus VHS case, it is the home video recording market. Each sale of a video recorder goes to one competitor or the other. If the sales for one competitor pull slightly ahead of the other, then the competitor gets more revenue. It can use this revenue for development or marketing, which in turn helps it get additional customers. In addition, supporting technologies go to the winning competitor, making it easier to use. At the same time, the rival gets less revenue, making it less able to compete until it is squeezed out. In the case of Beta versus VHS, each person who chooses VHS over Beta makes VHS more of a *de facto* standard for video recorders, giving it additional customers.

VHS initially pulled the system in its favor by investing heavily in content, especially movie titles (whereas Beta put more emphasis on the technology). As customers bought VHS for the movie titles, it became more and more of a standard, dominating Beta in the home recording market. As you can see in the diagram on the next page entitled "Success to the Successful Archetype: Beta and VHS," the old adage, "Them that's got gets" succinctly describes the dynamics of the success to the successful archetype.

Another way to think about this archetype is that the successful competitor's product becomes more valuable as more people switch to it. When one competitor gets ahead of the other, it becomes more attractive *because* it is more widely used. In this case, if more people are using VHS, new purchasers are more likely to buy it because they can exchange tapes with friends, they can more easily find pre-recorded tapes, and so on.

Success to the Successful Archetype: Beta and VHS

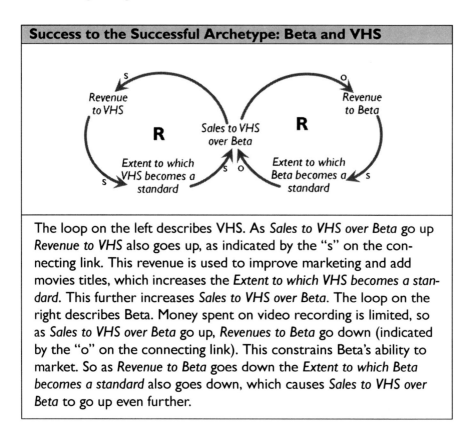

The loop on the left describes VHS. As *Sales to VHS over Beta* go up *Revenue to VHS* also goes up, as indicated by the "s" on the connecting link. This revenue is used to improve marketing and add movies titles, which increases the *Extent to which VHS becomes a standard*. This further increases *Sales to VHS over Beta*. The loop on the right describes Beta. Money spent on video recording is limited, so as *Sales to VHS over Beta* go up, *Revenues to Beta* go down (indicated by the "o" on the connecting link). This constrains Beta's ability to market. So as *Revenue to Beta* goes down the *Extent to which Beta becomes a standard* also goes down, which causes *Sales to VHS over Beta* to go up even further.

The same archetype applies to an organizational change—as more people use a new process or tool or software or team-based skill, it becomes more valuable. Consider a Supply Chain Management (SCM) program that is designed to manage customer orders from sale to delivery. As more aspects of order management move from the legacy system to the SCM system, there is more information on the SCM system. With more information on it, the SCM system is more useful, and so more people want their aspect of an order on it. The more the SCM system is used, the more useful it becomes. After it gets started, the momentum swings more and more away from the legacy system and toward the SCM system.

The More SCM Is Used, the More Valuable It Becomes

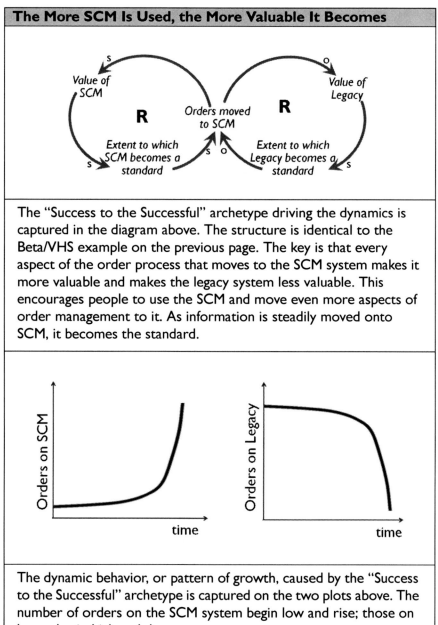

The "Success to the Successful" archetype driving the dynamics is captured in the diagram above. The structure is identical to the Beta/VHS example on the previous page. The key is that every aspect of the order process that moves to the SCM system makes it more valuable and makes the legacy system less valuable. This encourages people to use the SCM and move even more aspects of order management to it. As information is steadily moved onto SCM, it becomes the standard.

The dynamic behavior, or pattern of growth, caused by the "Success to the Successful" archetype is captured on the two plots above. The number of orders on the SCM system begin low and rise; those on legacy begin high and drop.

Of course, success is not inevitable. An initial push toward the SCM system is necessary to jump-start its reinforcing loop in the "Success to the Successful" archetype. Continued use of the SCM system is needed to reinforce it.

There are more examples of system archetypes applied to organizational change in Chapter 4. See "Shifting the Burden Applied to Mass Exposure" starting on page 110, or "Fixes that Fail Applied to Hire Advocates" starting on page 116.

Closing the Loop

In their bestseller, *The Fifth Discipline Fieldbook*, Senge, Ross, Kleiner, Roberts, and Smith argue that natural languages, such as English, influence our understanding of cause and effect. Subject-verb constructions help us understand "A causes B," but obscure our understanding of "A causes B and B causes A." Thus, natural language construction leads us to think of actions as being one-way rather than part of a feedback loop.

An ancient Japanese proverb illustrates the limits of linear thinking and the value of thinking systemically.[13] The proverb says, "When the wind blows, the demand for wooden buckets goes up." Like many Japanese proverbs, it is subtle and deserves explanation. When the wind blows, dust gets in the air. The dust gets in people's eyes, causing some of them to go blind. In ancient Japan, blind people typically become folk-tale singers, who accompanied themselves using a shamisen, a guitar-like instrument made with cat skin. So, as more people went blind, more cats were needed for the shamisens, and the number of cats went down. This caused the number of rats to increase. The rats like to chew on containers to see if there is anything to eat inside. When they chewed through a wooden bucket, it became useless since it could no longer hold water. So people bought new wooden buckets, causing the demand to go up, as illustrated below.

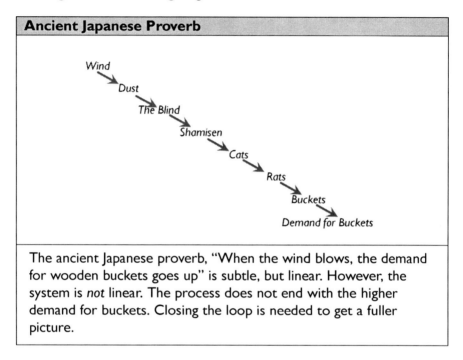

Ancient Japanese Proverb

Wind → Dust → The Blind → Shamisen → Cats → Rats → Buckets → Demand for Buckets

The ancient Japanese proverb, "When the wind blows, the demand for wooden buckets goes up" is subtle, but linear. However, the system is *not* linear. The process does not end with the higher demand for buckets. Closing the loop is needed to get a fuller picture.

The proverb is subtle; it is meant to call attention to unexpected down-stream outcomes. Despite its subtlety, it is linear. It fails to close the loop and reveal the full picture. When the demand for wooden buckets went up, bucket makers in ancient Japan cut down trees in the nearby forest to make buckets. With nearby trees cut down, towns were even less protected from the wind. So towns experienced more wind, causing more blind people, fewer cats, and more rats chewing on buckets. This reduced the number of buckets, which caused the demand for wooden buckets to increase even further. The linearity of the proverb misses the reinforcing loop that increased wind and dust and blindness. Contrast the diagram above with the systems view on the next page.

Ancient Japanese Proverb: Systems View

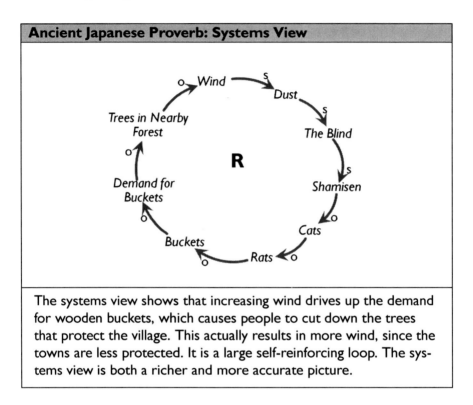

The systems view shows that increasing wind drives up the demand for wooden buckets, which causes people to cut down the trees that protect the village. This actually results in more wind, since the towns are less protected. It is a large self-reinforcing loop. The systems view is both a richer and more accurate picture.

Systems thinking is a disciplined methodology to show the big picture. Its language of links and loops provides a discipline to think in wholes rather than parts by describing how the parts interact to form wholes. This language demonstrates the role of time and the importance of feedback loops to the dynamics of the system. Systems thinking is part of what informs the Tipping Point model of change.

The next chapter puts together the ideas from Chapters 1 and 2 to see what lessons learned from public health and systems thinking can teach us about how to spread an idea.

Moving Forward

Key Concepts

❧ Systems thinking is a disciplined way to 1) think in wholes, rather than parts, 2) recognize the importance of time, and 3) understand the effects of closed feedback loops.

❧ The events that we experience are a result of system structure. All system structure can be defined in terms of balancing and reinforcing feedback loops. Balancing loops always create equilibrium, and reinforcing loops always create exponential growth or decline.

❧ There are a few structures (as described in the language of links and loops) that appear in many different contexts. In each context, these structures generate the same sort of behavior over time and are known as system archetypes.

Points to Ponder

❧ What opportunities do you have to step back and see the bigger systemic picture? Can you create such opportunities?

❧ Can you re-frame aspects of your change that you are thinking about linearly and find the feedback loops that are driving them?

❧ How can you harness the power of two in your organizational change?

Chapter 3

Making Change Contagious

> A dwarf on a giant's shoulders sees the farther of the two.
> —George Herbert

T he Tipping Point model provides a dynamic view of implementing an organizational change initiative. It uses the facts
that implementation is a process that evolves over time, and
organizations change when people in them change. People whose
attitude toward an initiative has progressed from disconnected to
committed influence others. Committed employees adopt the
behaviors necessary to achieve the business value from an organizational change. The Tipping Point model builds on the models
outlined in Chapter 1, and it leverages systems thinking and
concepts from public health. The model helps leaders understand
the factors that can create a positive epidemic of commitment and
enthusiasm for an organizational change.

The Tipping Point Framework

> You cannot plan the future by the past.
> —Edmund Burke

Like any model in business, the purpose of the Tipping Point is to improve results, in this case by improving implementation of an organizational change effort. The effort may seek to make products or production more sustainable, boost sales and revenue, upgrade processes or technology, get new products to market faster, decrease costs, increase productivity, promote quality, improve customer satisfaction, reduce accidents, or otherwise enhance profits. Whatever the goal, the Tipping Point model concentrates on creating contagious commitment to it. The model provides the common vocabulary and concepts needed to implement change. It highlights actions leaders can take to make a change contagious and sustainable, provides the underpinning to make implementation plans more strategic, and enables participants to discuss and evaluate progress.

Much of the background for the Tipping Point has been described in previous chapters. See "Organizational Change Is about People" beginning on page 12 to review the four attitudes toward an organizational change: Advocates, Incubators, Apathetics, and Resisters. "Supporting Change" (beginning on page 31) goes over the two types of support: People and Environmental Support. This chapter reviews the attitudes toward change, and describes how leaders can engender support by introducing seven "levers of change." Each lever of change is defined and examples of using them are given. The following chapter takes an even closer look at how the levers of change interact with each other—sometimes to create more leverage and sometimes in ways that can be dangerous.

Four Attitudes Define Four Pools of People

As mentioned in Chapter 1, at any point in time all the people in the organization fall into one of four groups depending on their attitude toward the change. Advocates have experience with the change that has demonstrated its value to them. Incubators have heard about the change, but they are not yet sure whether it will work in their situation. Resisters are pushing back against the change—either covertly or overtly. Apathetics feel disconnected from the change. Either they have not heard about it or believe that it will not affect them. (The four attitude pools are summarized in "Four Groups or Pools of People in the Tipping Point Model" on the following page.) The people who are in each of these four groups can and do switch between them. As a leader, you want to turn as many as possible into Advocates of the change, because without a positive attitude toward a change it is unlikely that employees will embrace the new behaviors, methodologies, and technology that it requires. You want to reach a critical mass of Advocates (see "Critical Mass" on page 38) so that the change reaches a tipping point and people flow naturally into the Advocates pool.

It is easy to underestimate the power of apathy and to overestimate the effect of resistance. In a *Harvard Business Review* article, "Campaigning for Change," Larry Hirschhorn says that most change initiatives fail not from resistance or insufficient funds, but because people simply stop paying attention to them. That is, initiatives fail from apathy; they are ignored to death. The Tipping Point model places its emphasis on moving people away from apathy toward incubating the change and then on supporting them to become and remain Advocates.

Attitudes are contagious. A positive, committed attitude toward a change can spread from one employee to another, leading to effective implementation and positive financial results for the organiza-

Four Groups or Pools of People in the Tipping Point Model

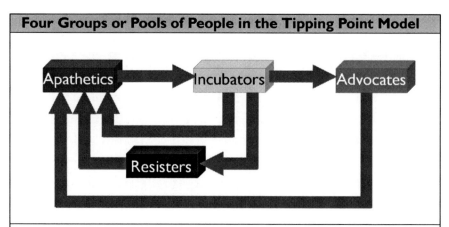

Everyone in an organization falls into one of four groups or pools of people, depending on their attitude toward a change at any given time. As their attitude evolves, they move between the pools.

Advocates—Advocates are people whose experience in the change leads them to believe that it will make a positive difference. They are interested in sharing their own expertise and enthusiasm with others—in the hope of making the implementation of the change successful.

Incubators—Incubators are thinking about the change, but they are not sure if they believe that it will work or if management is fully behind it. They are thinking and learning about the concepts behind the change and comparing these concepts against their experience with how work gets done in their organization.

Apathetics—People are Apathetic if they have not heard of the change or simply disregard it. Based on previous experience, many people believe they can ignore a change and it will go away, as it often has in the past. Such people make up the Apathetics pool.

Resisters—Resisters oppose the change. Resisters who openly and actively challenge the change can be an important source of information. Their concerns may represent potential roadblocks that need to be addressed. On the other hand, people who are covertly undermining the change are often a dangerous hindrance to success.

tion. A negative, destructive attitude can also spread, with potentially disastrous consequences. Unfortunately, negative attitudes about the change tend to spread more easily than positive ones, and can undermine a change that is critical for your organization's success. *Perceived* value and clear support for a change are key. In Everett Rogers's words, "… perceptions of the attributes of an innovation, not the attributes as classified by experts or change agents, affect its rate of adoption."[12] Attitudes toward a change program are shaped by the benefit or the burden that employees *believe* the program will bring, combined with the level of support (or lack of it) that they *experience*.

Employees' perceived value of a change and the level and type of support interact in predictable ways. A well-supported change that is perceived as a benefit to the organization is obviously the most likely to succeed. At the opposite end is a change that is perceived as a burden (even if it has potential to be a benefit) and is not well supported by leadership. Such a change is almost certainly doomed. A negative attitude toward such a change is sure to spread quickly through the organization. If employees perceive a change as worthwhile but don't see it supported, then it is important to find ways to increase the support for employees to make the change. If the change is perceived as a burden, find out why. It could be a valid and fixable problem with the change itself, or it may be that the business case needs to be made more clearly. The table titled "Perceived Value and Support Drive Attitudes toward a Change" on the following page summarizes the relationship of management support and perceived value of a change.

"Fair process," defined by Kim and Mauborgne in the *Harvard Business Review,* can improve the perception of the burden or benefit of a change. Their research has shown that "individuals are most likely to trust and cooperate freely with systems — whether they themselves win or lose by those systems — when fair process is observed." People tend to be just as concerned with the fairness

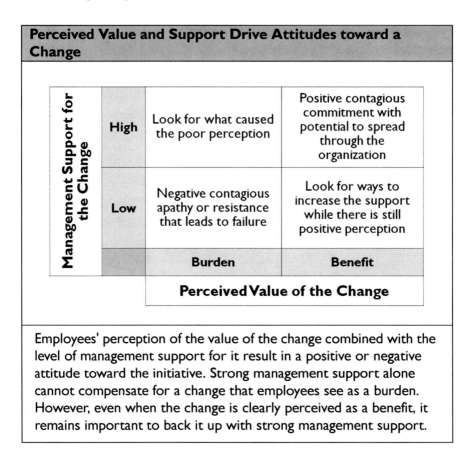

Perceived Value and Support Drive Attitudes toward a Change

		Burden	Benefit
Management Support for the Change	**High**	Look for what caused the poor perception	Positive contagious commitment with potential to spread through the organization
	Low	Negative contagious apathy or resistance that leads to failure	Look for ways to increase the support while there is still positive perception

Perceived Value of the Change

Employees' perception of the value of the change combined with the level of management support for it result in a positive or negative attitude toward the initiative. Strong management support alone cannot compensate for a change that employees see as a burden. However, even when the change is clearly perceived as a benefit, it remains important to back it up with strong management support.

of the process as with the fairness of the outcome. Kim and Mauborgne define three principles of fair process: *engagement, explanation,* and *expectation clarity. Engagement* means involving people in decisions that affect them by encouraging discussion and examination of assumptions. Management has the responsibility of making the decisions, after which *explanation* is needed to ensure that everyone affected by the decision understands the reasoning behind it. Once the decision is made, there are new rules and *expectations,* and it is incumbent on management to make these expectations clear to all who are affected. Fair process is not consensus or majority rule. It is about employee involvement, management sincerity, and process transparency to induce a fair perception of a change

Recall Medical Machines, the firm described in Chapter 1: "Spreading Good Ideas" that developed a new product line in response to competition from start-ups. The sales force lacked experience with the new products, so Medical Machines implemented a knowledge management (KM) system in an attempt to overcome poor communication between sales and engineering. At the same time that Medical Machines was implementing the KM system, it was involved in another organizational change. Medical Machines had to maintain their standard of attracting and retaining the most talented employees. The pool of potential new employees with the skills that Medical Machines needed was becoming more diverse. To present a positive work environment for this new talent, it recognized the need to increase its own diversity. Below is a description of their experience in implementing the diversity initiative.

A Diversity Initiative at Medical Machines

There were two main business drivers of the initiative to increase diversity at Medical Machines and two smaller motivators. First, the demographics of the potential new employee pool were growing more diverse (becoming more variable in gender, race, country of origin, and sexual orientation). If Medical Machines expected to both attract and retain the most talented people from this pool, they needed to present a positive work environment for them. Second, the face of their customer base was changing. In Medical Machines' traditional market, hospitals were also drawing their new hires from the same diverse talent pool. So customers who were making the buying decisions on medical test equipment were also more diverse. At the same time, Medical Machines was selling more in the global market, further increasing the diversity of the customers. There were also two smaller motivators for the diversity program—one reactive and one proactive. On the reactive side, Medical Machines supplied laboratory test equipment to military and veterans hospitals, and it feared that in the future the government might impose diversity quotas on suppliers. On the proactive side, many managers within Medical

Machines recognized that diverse teams simply outperformed homogeneous teams. Diverse teams represented many different viewpoints and thus more creativity.

The director of the diversity program understood the importance of Advocates, so she formalized the Advocate network. She created a description of the skills, interests, and experience needed to advocate for a "flexible, inclusive, motivating environment for maximum contribution." People applied to join the formal Advocate network. Advocates agreed to give 10% of their time to the network before they were accepted into it. The group met for a five-day residential training to kickoff the program.

To get the information needed to accomplish the vision, they heard from experts in racism, gender, sexual orientation, foreign customs, and language differences as applied to business. They were trained to proactively identify and deal with problems, as well as in team building. There were monthly Advocate teleconferences to keep people together, share success stories, and deal with challenges. The Advocate network named themselves "strategic termites," because their goal was eating away at the dead wood of wrong-headed ideas on diversity so that new ones had room to grow.

Resistance to the diversity program was a definite reality. One source of resistance came from executives who did not understand the business case and confused the initiative with compliance to government mandates. To overcome this resistance the diversity director enlisted the help of a senior vice-president of sales who thoroughly understood and realized the significance of the business case. He had been with Medical Machines for many years. During his tenure, he had established a successful reputation in sales and marketing, and was responsible for some key accounts. Because he was a white male, most of the executive team could identify with him, and they felt they understood his motivation. He put himself on executive team meetings' agendas to lay out the business case for diversity. He spoke privately with peers on the changing face of their customers and listened to their concerns.

Before long, everyone on the executive team understood the business case, and resistance at the executive level was greatly reduced, if not eliminated. Dealing with this major barrier early on was important to their success. Resistance at lower levels of the hierarchy was just as real. Several approaches were used to address this resistance. The first approach centered on constant honesty. Frankness and candor in describing the problems of a homogeneous workforce and the long road to attaining diversity were key. This demanded honestly admitting mistakes in implementation and demonstrating a willingness to rectify them. A second approach to removing resistance involved managing expectations. It is not unusual for diversity programs to expose problems that have affected performance, but which have been hidden. Exposing these problems is part of addressing them; however, it can make things appear worse before they improve. Everyone needs to be educated to expect this "worse before better" outcome, which is common to many change initiatives. (See "The Path to Change is Rarely Straight or Smooth" on page 33.) The third method was more direct. In some departments, diversity criteria in hiring, promotion, and education were added to managers' goals and used in their annual reviews. This raised awareness, and helped managers connect the business case for diversity to their other work.

Turning Apathetics into Incubators was mainly done through direct contact between members of the strategic termite network of Advocates and other employees. There were also other efforts focused on keeping diversity on employees' "radar screen," and giving them information on what to expect. The Advocates offered voluntary, day-long courses in diversity. The Medical Machines company newspaper ran articles on the value that diversity brought to the business and on executive commitment to it. Over time this resulted in growing numbers of Advocates, some of whom eventually joined the strategic termite network.

All four attitude pools are represented in the diversity initiative at Medical Machines. To make the initiative stick, management's initial challenge was to create the environment in which most people fully perceived the value that it could bring. Then they had to champion the change so that people would become Advocates of it and it could spread. The seven levers of change, described next, are the means to create this informed, supportive environment.

Levers of Change

> The key to successful leadership today is influence, not authority.
> —Ken Blanchard

Each of the seven levers of change in the Tipping Point model represents a wide range of related, specific actions that management can take to affect people's willingness to embrace a change. These actions are called levers of change because, just as a lever and fulcrum give a mechanical advantage *when used properly,* these seven levers of change give an implementation advantage when changing an organization. The specific actions represented by a lever vary from organization to organization and from change to change. In one situation a particular lever may be very powerful, while in another it may be counterproductive. However, for every change all seven levers must be understood and *considered.*

There are two types of levers: People-Support and Environmental-Support levers. Each People-Support lever has a single, direct effect (for example, to move people from Apathetics to Incubators). The Environmental-Support levers have an indirect effect on all of the movement between attitude pools. The four People-Support levers are **Contacts** between Advocates and Apathetics, **Mass Exposure, Hire Advocates**, and **Shift Resisters**. The three Environmental-Support levers are **Walk the Talk, Reward & Recognition**, and **Infrastructure**. There is a quick summary of the two types of support and their respective levers in "The Tipping Point's Seven Levers of Change" on page 83.

People-Support Levers

Contacts are opportunities that Advocates have to share their experience and enthusiasm for the change with people who feel disconnected from it. Contacts are often casual one-to-one

The Tipping Point's Seven Levers of Change	
People-Support Levers	*Environmental-Support Levers*
• Contacts between Advocates and Apathetics • Mass Exposure • Hire Advocates • Shift Resisters	• Infrastructure • Walk the Talk • Reward & Recognition
Each People-Support lever directly affects the flow between one attitude pool and another. Environmental-Support levers have an indirect effect on the movement between all the pools. To understand the distinction between People- and Environmental-Support levers, an analogy of pouring wine from a barrel might be useful. People-Support levers are like a spigot. The more you open a spigot, the faster the wine flows. Environmental-Support levers are like tilting the barrel; tilting changes the environment so that for the same spigot position, there is more flow or less flow (depending on which way the barrel is tilted). Opening the spigot has a direct effect on the flow, and tilting the barrel is changing the environment to affect the flow indirectly. Two key concepts underlie the Tipping Point model: 1) people moving or flowing between pools as their attitude toward a change evolves and 2) leaders using levers to cause or affect the rate of movement.	

meetings in the hallway, but they can include more formal meetings. The key to contacts is that they must provide *two-way communication* between the Advocates and Apathetics. This distinguishes contacts from Mass Exposure. The inherent feedback in Contacts can provide a mechanism to learn about concerns that Apathetics may have about the change or its implementation and for Advocates to express their enthusiasm for it.

Mass Exposure provides a way to introduce the change by using posters, web pages, mass emails, logo mugs and other trinkets, one-size-fits-all awareness training, or other means designed to give groups of people information about the change. Mass Exposure does not provide for any feedback from the people who are the targets of the change. Mass Exposure is a way to let people know facts and plans about the change, but it cannot uncover employees' concerns about it. Nor can it provide a platform for Advocates to explain their own experience with the change.

The third People-Support lever is **Hire Advocates**, which affects the flow into the Advocates pool. In businesses, hiring and attrition are going on all the time. The Hire Advocates lever represents hiring that is over and above hiring people for job skill or succession or growth. People hired via this lever are hired specifically because they are Advocates; they have expertise, experience, and enthusiasm for the change initiative, and would not have been hired were it not for the initiative. For example, a firm implementing an enterprise resource planning (ERP) program to manage orders, manufacturing, and order fulfillment hired people from a different industry who had experience customizing ERP's. If the firm had not been implementing an ERP system that needed to be customize, these employees would not have been hired.

Shift Resisters is the fourth and final People-Support lever of change. It may be necessary to move Resisters to a department that is not affected by the change, to give them assignments more consistent with their beliefs, or perhaps to remove them from the company. Shift Resisters can also include changing the implementation plan so that groups that are resistant will not be affected until after the change's value is established.[14] I worked with a team who changed their rollout plan for a new payroll system to affect union members later in the schedule. After working with the Tipping Point simulation, the team felt that the union would feel more supported, and thus be more supportive, if they saw success with the new system in other areas and knew that they were not the guinea pigs for a new system.

"Examples of the People-Support Levers," on page 86, uses a customer relationship management (CRM) program to illustrate examples of the People-Support Levers.

Environmental-Support Levers

Environmental Support is as important as People Support. Although its effect on attitudes is indirect, without it even the most critical change for an organization is likely to fail. The Tipping Point looks at the effects of three key Environmental-Support levers of change: Infrastructure, Walk the Talk, and Reward & Recognition.

Every change program requires some sort of **Infrastructure**, which could include hardware, software, facilities, processes, or manuals, and will be different for each program. For example, merging two business units could require modifications to compensation plans, new HR policies and manuals, and perhaps focused job-specific training to help the business units understand each other's product lines or processes. Implementing a supply chain management system could require software and workstations. There is always an ideal amount of Infrastructure to support a change. However, in the real world, there are also budget constraints, forcing decisions about how much of the ideal infrastructure to invest in. The Infrastructure lever represents the proportion of the ideal infrastructure for the change that you are willing to invest in.

A participant in a Tipping Point workshop described an example of the reality of investing in less than the ideal amount of Infrastructure. She was working with a Fortune 100 company that was doing a major overhaul of its benefits package. Investing in 100% of the ideal Infrastructure would mean greatly expanding their automated call distribution (ACD) system and obtaining new workstations for the human resources (HR) staff who were respon-

Examples of the People-Support Levers

While the specifics the levers in different changes will vary, examples can make the levers more concrete. Consider implementing a Customer Relationship Management (CRM) system. CRM systems maintain historical and current customer data. Well-designed CRM systems provide a window into customer needs. They allow better customer service and improved sales by providing detailed customer data to the employee who needs it. The following examples are ways that the four People-Support levers of change could be used in implementing a CRM system.

Contacts between Advocates and Apathetics—There are a number of ways that Advocates could share their experience of a CRM with those who are Apathetic. For example, effective salespeople with experience in CRM can explain how the information on customers that was available in the CRM database helped them make sales. Or customer support people can explain how it helped them find trends in problems reported by customers which in turn made them more effective in supporting customers.

Mass Exposure—A CRM would probably require general awareness training to ensure that everyone knows what CRM means and broadly what to expect from it. A web page with more detail could supplement the training. Articles with examples from other companies or divisions on the benefits they realized with CRM could be useful. Trinkets, such as logo mugs and T-shirts, might also be helpful, but only if they are matched by serious Environmental Support (see next section).

Hire Advocates—Hiring an Advocate of CRM from an unrelated business, who would not normally be hired for job skill or succession or growth, might be necessary if it is done prudently. For example, a company with no CRM expertise might hire people with knowledge of the technical side of implementing a CRM, even if their experience is in a different business.

Shift Resisters—If the sales force is resisting the change, the implementation could begin with customer service. When Resisters see the value of CRM, they are more likely to come on board. If a key leader is among the Resisters, it is important to understand why and either address the source of the resistance (if possible) or remove the person from the key position.

sible for answering questions about the new benefits. After the benefit system was implemented, the additional ACD components and workstations would no longer be needed. The firm's management felt that they simply could not justify the expense for Infrastructure that had such a short shelf life, no matter how valuable it was during the implementation. Instead they invested in a comprehensive web page that could answer many employees' inquiries and would remain useful after the implementation was completed. The web page reduced the number of calls to HR asking for particulars on the new benefits plan but did not eliminate them. Without the expanded ACD, employees got more busy signals when calling HR than the firm wanted. In the end, although the solution was less than ideal and had an effect on the implementation, the firm felt it was a cost-effective compromise.

Walk the Talk refers to leading by example. Leadership is more than having authority, it requires setting the standard, or in Mahatma Gandhi's words, "being the change you want to see." In business, this means taking advantage of opportunities to lead that are consistent with the change. Examples of Walk the Talk are making the business case clear, surfacing employees' concerns, aligning the management team, setting standards for rewarding success, or monitoring progress and adjusting the course when necessary. On the other hand, expecting subordinates to provide all the leadership or not using the data it creates in decision making is *not* Walk the Talk. For example, trying to lead a quality initiative without including quality metrics in product development reviews is the opposite of Walk the Talk. The Walk the Talk lever represents the proportion of opportunities that leaders have to exemplify the change that they actually take advantage of. A leader who is serious about a change will not only *use* every available opening to exemplify the change, she will *craft* more.

Reward & Recognition includes monetary incentives and formal and informal recognition for support of the change. The range of

Reward & Recognition is broad: it includes raises, bonuses, and/or stock options as well as giving credit through an award, a thank-you note, or a public pat on the back. Rewarding and recognizing individuals and teams who support a change emphasizes the importance of the change to the organization. Obviously, any firm needs to reward and recognize many things. So the proportion of the Reward & Recognition that is devoted to a given change should reflect the importance of the change relative to numerous other activities for which employees should be also rewarded and recognized.

Examples of the Environmental-Support Levers

Continuing with the CRM system begun on page 86, the following are illustrations of the three Environmental-Support levers of change.

Infrastructure—Every CRM needs customized software and per-haps hardware. There also may be job-specific training so that people know how to use the CRM tools effectively. Job-specific training is tailored to a person's responsibilities, so that the sales force would get different training than the customer service staff. (This is in contrast to the generic training that is part of Mass Exposure.)

Walk the Talk—There are many ways to lead by example with a CRM. Examples of Walk the Talk include clarifying and dissemi-nating the business case to all stakeholders to create buy-in for the CRM, making sure that company systems (i.e., compensation, operational reviews, business strategy) are aligned with the CRM, ensuring that everyone hears about instances where the CRM was a benefit to the company, and encouraging use of the CRM over the legacy system whenever possible.

Reward & Recognition—Rewards include raises and bonuses for both implementers and users of the system. Recognition includes handwritten thank-you notes to implementers or formal awards for sales or customer service people for applying the CRM infor-mation in novel and useful ways.

The Levers of Change and the Pools Interact

How do the seven levers interact with the four attitudes that employees may have toward the change? First consider the People-Support levers. Both Contacts with Advocates and Mass Exposure have the *potential* to move people from Apathetic to Incubator. That is, under the right conditions, either lever can cause people to investigate the change and the strengths it may have. This is not to say that both levers are equally effective or that neither has side effects. From Incubators, people can enter the Advocates pool if they recognize the value of the change and the support for it. Hire Advocates provides a second entry into the Advocates pool. Shift Resisters has the immediate effect of reducing the numbers in the pool of Resisters. The relative effectiveness and side effects of all of these levers are discussed in Chapter 4.

The three Environmental-Support levers create the atmosphere to sustain the change. In essence, they make the People-Support levers more—or less—effective. If Environmental Support is high, then people tend to spend less time incubating the change before getting the experience needed to become Advocates; low Environmental Support has the opposite effect. Similarly, high Environmental Support makes Contacts between Advocates and Apathetics more effective (which means more likely to change Apathetics into Incubators). Environmental Support can also mitigate some of the undesirable side effects of hiring Advocates from the outside. In general, Environmental-Support levers, when properly used, provide the underpinning that makes the change work.

In addition to these three levers of change, Population Mix also influences Environmental Support. Population Mix is the proportion of people in the organization who are Advocates. Advocates learn from each other and provide a mutual support network. The more Advocates in the organization, the easier it is for an individual to remain an Advocate and to encourage others to become Advocates. So the higher the Population Mix (i.e., the higher the proportion of Advocates), the more supportive the environment is to the change. Conversely, more Apathetics lowers the Population Mix and has a negative effect on Environmental Support. The Population Mix is part of the context that can be either conducive or hostile toward an organizational change. Thus, it is the fourth input to Environmental Support, but it is not a lever of change because it does not represent an action that leaders can take.

The diagram on the following page, "The Tipping Point Model of Change: Key Components" gives the structure of the model and its major components. It adds the seven levers of change to the diagram of the four attitude pools previously shown in "Four Groups or Pools of People in the Tipping Point Model" on page 76. The diagram shows where each lever has its major effect. For example, Contacts and Mass Exposure both affect the flow from Apathetics to Incubators. The three Environmental-Support levers and the Population Mix affect overall Environmental Support, which in turn has an effect on the flows between pools.

Major Effects of the Seven Levers of Change

In the early stages of a change initiative, Advocates are similar to the innovators described in the diffusion of innovation model outlined by Everett Rogers. (See "Critical Mass" beginning on page 38 or, for more detail, see Appendix 1: "More on Models of Change.") They have enthusiasm for the change that they are eager to share. When they talk with Apathetics, some of the Apathetics will begin to consider the ideas behind the change and become Incubators, and then go through the transition stages described by William Bridges. (See "Aligning the Organization

The Tipping Point Model of Change: Key Components

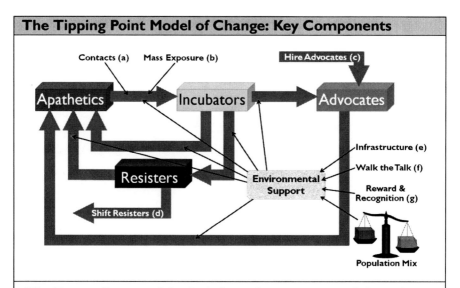

The Tipping Point model is built from the interaction of eleven basic components: four attitudes toward a change and seven levers of change. The four attitudes represent four possible mind-sets which any member of the organization can have toward the change at any given time. The four attitude pools are Apathetics, Incubators, Resisters, and Advocates. As people's attitude toward the change evolves, they move between the four pools, as illustrated by the wide gray arrows.

The seven levers of change are actions that leaders can take to affect people's attitude toward a change. The seven levers in the Tipping Point model are: (a) Contacts between Advocates and Apathetics; (b) Mass Exposure; (c) Hire Advocates; (d) Shift Resisters; (e) Infrastructure; (f) Walk the Talk; and (g) Reward & Recognition. People-Support levers (a–d) directly affect a single flow, into or out of an attitude pool. Environmental-Support levers (e–g) affect the context for the change and thus have an indirect affect on all the flows. The thin black arrows indicate where the levers have an influence on people moving between the attitude pools.

The structure of the model describes the relationship between the attitude pools and the seven levers of change. Applying the model means using the levers together with attention to how all the components interact. This means knowing which of the levers are "must have" and which can only be used with great caution as well as when to apply each lever. It also means adapting the model to individual changes and unique corporate cultures.

and Guiding the Change" on page 42, or, for more detail, see Appendix 1: "More on Models of Change.") They begin letting go of their old ideas about how work gets done and begin considering new ones. They have to deal with the ambiguity of giving up familiar ways of working while being unsure of precisely what the new ways will be like, how effective they will be, and so on. Incubation cannot be rushed. It takes time to consider the value of new ideas and to learn and try out new processes. This is all part of Incubation.

Employees can move from Apathetics to Incubators in a second way—through Mass Exposure. Classes or information sessions, mass emails or voicemails, or even posters are examples of Mass Exposure. They can inform people about a change. Information alone can cause some Apathetics to think seriously about the new change initiative. It is unlikely that the same proportion of people will begin incubating after Mass Exposure as do after Contact with an Advocate, where they hear firsthand experience and can ask questions. On the other hand, Mass Exposure can reach more people at once. These people will also begin the transition process described by Bridges, which initiates the Incubation process.

Once people have become Incubators they take one of three paths: 1) They can say to themselves, "This isn't for me, not in this organization," and go back to the Apathetics pool; 2) The change can resonate with their experience and values so they become Advocates; 3) They may begin to resist the change, believing it to be counterproductive or inconsistent with their beliefs or how they view the organization. Which of these paths the Incubators take depends on the level of Environmental Support for the change—more support tends to make more Advocates. Also, depending on the support for the change, Resisters may continue to resist or they may become Apathetic again.

Advocates cannot be taken for granted. Initially, Advocates' own enthusiasm may mask a lack of sponsorship for a change. Without a leader sponsoring an organizational change, it is unlikely to succeed. (In *Managing at the Speed of Change*, Daryl Conner outlines this trap, and there is more on it in Appendix 1: "More on Models of Change.") If Advocates doubt the sponsorship, as evidenced by a lack of Environmental Support, they may decide that there is no real advantage for them to continue contributing to the change. They will go back into the Apathetics pool or leave the company.

In Chapter 1, Dan Siems began relating his experience using the Tipping Point at Endevco Corporation. (See "Process Improvement on the Factory Floor" on page 14.) Recall that Endevco designed and developed sensors for extreme environments with a wide range of industrial applications. The firm needed to improve the processes in the factory to decrease variation and reduce costs. The Operations group was charged with the change. The Factory Physics approach they chose challenged the familiar ways of working of other stakeholders, in particular Manufacturing, Sales and Marketing, and Planning. Thus, they each had very different attitudes toward the change. Dan's example helps illustrate how a sponsor, in this case the VP of Operations, can use the seven levers of change to affect those attitudes.

Process Improvement on the Factory Floor, Concluded

After spending time exploring the Tipping Point model through a facilitated workshop, the VP of Operations better under-stood how to bring people on board to implement Factory Physics concepts and reduce inventories. He began by keeping the inner group of change leaders small. This facilitated maximum one-on-one contact and allowed a nexus of thought to develop around Factory Physics concepts and application. The phrase, "keep the team together" described his determination to learn, digest, and incorporate these new ideas as a team. This small group slowly moved from Apathetics to Incubators and finally to Advocates as they worked at applying the relationships between cycle time, work in progress, throughput, and variation to their operation.

Because the group was small, the VP was better able to lead by example, dealing with any Resisters in an open, non-threatening way by promoting dialogue and the exchange of ideas. From these close-knit gatherings, Environmental Support needs were determined early. The necessary Infrastructure was identified to sustain the newly realized behaviors. The development of data extraction and analysis software was identified as a key infrastructure need that was quickly filled. Reward & Recognition became intrinsic through released cash, better customer service, less expediting, and faster cycles of learning. The desire to reduce inventories became an incentive to change.

The VP of Operations continued to Walk the Talk and expected the same from the small group of change leaders. For example, when faced with a decision to expedite a request from an important customer, the team looked to the VP of Operations. Together they debated creative, doable alternatives, but decided that, in this case, expediting this job was the best decision. They had the Tipping Point model to guide their positioning. Without the model, they would never have discussed the expedite as a team; instead they would have blamed the VP for failing to Walk the Talk or Factory Physics for not being applicable. Their debate remained "healthy" because The Tipping Point model gave them a frame of reference for discussion. It built them up as a team and turned them into thinking Advocates. They applied Factory Physics in a rational way, acknowledging that sometimes you can't have "the ideal" but need to work with "less than ideal"—which does not make you any less of an Advocate. The entire team took responsibility for the decision to expedite the job, and everyone understood why!

As the small Advocates pool continued to gain expertise, the VP helped the change leaders work with various parts of the organization—peers and superiors—to move them from Apathetics to Incubators. From the Tipping Point simulation, the VP knew that resistance is not innate and that Resisters are "built" when their needs and concerns are ignored. With stakes this high, there was no shortage of concerns. The VP met resistance with the mindset: "Resistance is good!", incorporating the Resisters' ideas where appropriate and using resistance as an opportunity to teach and gain alignment. These one-on-one engagements with Resisters proved extremely effective in removing the mythology surrounding how inventories were controlled.

With previous improvement initiatives, the VP would announce "the latest change" in an "All Hands" meeting. This time, the Mass Exposure lever was set and locked at zero—no announcements heralding a new era in inventory management were made. This avoided two things: 1) The "flash in the pan" syndrome—a big announcement with insufficient follow-up; 2) Resentment being built from within, "Why should we believe them now? Changes haven't worked in the past." At the same time, the Advocates pool worked hard to "convert" only those people they felt were critical to the change.

After a short time, the inventory control system was understood in light of the Factory Physics, so that when it came time to act, only a few strategic policy changes were needed to cause inventories to drop quickly. The operations group met the cash objective, improved on time delivery, and cut operating costs. They actually eliminated overtime! In addition, the rest of the organization "calmed down" and adopted a "daily pace" instead of the usual end of week surge needed to make their commitments. The inventory reduction campaign happened—all in the background— and continues to happen as the organization subordinates itself to a few policy changes and added metrics.

The inventory reduction results at Endevco were so successful that they got the attention of the Meggitt corporate directors— who asked them to teach other sites their secrets. The roll-out plan includes both Factory Physics, to manage the factory side of change, AND the Tipping Point model, to manage the people side of change, with an emphasis that BOTH are needed to create lasting, meaningful new ways of working.

—Dan Siems

From Dan's narrative, you can see that the VP of Operations understood how to leverage the Tipping Point model of change. He realized that over time the attitudes and actions of the people toward Factory Physics would evolve, depending not only on the inherent value of Factory Physics change itself, but on the stake-holders' support for it. He carefully balanced the seven levers of change and encouraged other leaders to do the same, thus creating an environment that fostered the spread of commitment toward improving the factory processes. Change is a process. The "right" values for the organization and for the change will vary with the change, the organization, and the phase in implementation. Being aware of the levers and their implications and balancing them according to the situation to construct an environment conducive to change demands constant attention and a willingness to adjust.

How Fast an Idea Is Spreading: The Tipping Ratio

> Success is never final.
> —Winston Churchill

Imagine that your brother-in-law just inherited a state-of-the-art sports club. Wanting to increase profit by increasing membership, he initiates a huge membership drive. He has fallen into a trap that many sports clubs have fallen into: offering huge incentives to his staff to sign up new members and focusing on bringing in new members without investigating what would make his existing members renew their membership each year. This could leave him with lots of new members, few renewals, and huge expenses for advertising and incentive programs.

It is an easy trap to fall into. Mobile phone service, cable, and long distance providers use similar tactics to get new customers and take the old ones for granted. It also happens in change manage-ment. It is easy just to focus on getting new Advocates—by encouraging Incubators to become Advocates (or perhaps by hiring them from the outside). However, if existing Advocates are not supported, they become former Advocates—typically by moving into the Apathetics pool (or by leaving the company).

Spending time, energy, and money to get Incubators to become Advocates while ignoring the outflow of Advocates into the Apathetics pool creates a compound problem. The Advocates pool doesn't grow in size and the people in it have less experience with the change, since the experienced Advocates have become discouraged and apathetic. The newer Advocates have less expertise to share with others, so they are less effective as Advocates.

The **tipping ratio** is a simple measure of how fast an idea is spreading that takes into account both new Advocates and people who lose interest and become former Advocates. It is the ratio of new Advocates to former Advocates, that is, the ratio of the number of people entering the Advocates pool (typically from Incubators) to the number leaving it (typically to flow into the Apathetics pool).

$$\text{tipping ratio} = \frac{\text{new Advocates}}{\text{former Advocates}}$$

A quick thought experiment illustrates the tipping ratio. Suppose at a given point in time there are 1000 Advocates for a particular change. If 100 new people become Advocates each week and 100 people lose interest and become Apathetics, then the tipping ratio would be 1.0 (100/100 = 1.0). The size of the Advocates pool would remain the same; there would be different Advocates, but their number would remain the same. Over time this change would become stagnant. If 99 people become new Advocates and 100 people lose interest and become former Advocates, then the tipping ratio would be 0.99 (99/100 = 0.99) and the Advocates pool would with time slowly dwindle to nothing. If there are 101 new Advocates and 100 former Advocates, then the tipping ratio would be 1.01. The change will spread, but it will spread slowly. However, if there are 99 or 100 or 101 new Advocates and only 1 person loses interest and becomes a former Advocate, then the tipping ratio would be around 100. This would indicate a positive epidemic of change that is spreading very quickly. Any time the tipping ratio is above 1, then the idea is spreading; if it is a lot greater than 1, then the idea is spreading very rapidly.

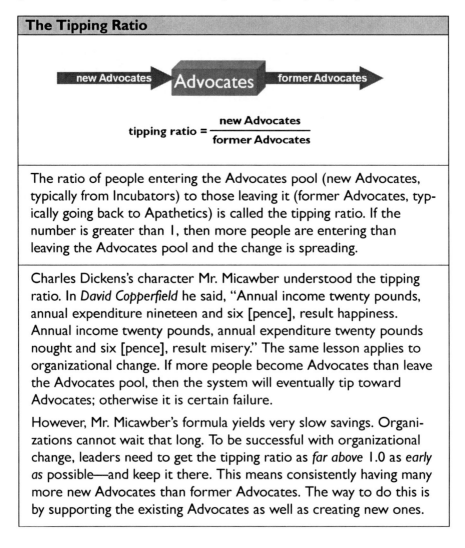

The Tipping Ratio

$$\text{tipping ratio} = \frac{\text{new Advocates}}{\text{former Advocates}}$$

The ratio of people entering the Advocates pool (new Advocates, typically from Incubators) to those leaving it (former Advocates, typically going back to Apathetics) is called the tipping ratio. If the number is greater than 1, then more people are entering than leaving the Advocates pool and the change is spreading.

Charles Dickens's character Mr. Micawber understood the tipping ratio. In *David Copperfield* he said, "Annual income twenty pounds, annual expenditure nineteen and six [pence], result happiness. Annual income twenty pounds, annual expenditure twenty pounds nought and six [pence], result misery." The same lesson applies to organizational change. If more people become Advocates than leave the Advocates pool, then the system will eventually tip toward Advocates; otherwise it is certain failure.

However, Mr. Micawber's formula yields very slow savings. Organizations cannot wait that long. To be successful with organizational change, leaders need to get the tipping ratio as *far above* 1.0 as *early as* possible—and keep it there. This means consistently having many more new Advocates than former Advocates. The way to do this is by supporting the existing Advocates as well as creating new ones.

The purpose of introducing the tipping ratio is to demonstrate that simply getting new Advocates is not enough. An idea spreading in a population depends just as much on taking care and keeping up the enthusiasm of the Advocates who already believe in the change and know that it's useful. Adapting an old adage from marketing underlines the importance of the tipping ratio: get Advocates, keep Advocates, and grow Advocates. The tipping ratio speaks to getting and keeping Advocates—both are absolutely fundamental to spreading a change within an organization. It is also important to constantly develop the Advocates' capacity to advocate a change. (See "Skilled Advocates" on page 40.) The more skillful Advocates are at spreading the change the better their morale and the more effective they will be at spreading acceptance for the new organizational change.

How can you tell if you are getting, keeping, and growing Advocates of your organization's change and which levers are making a difference for you? This was the question that Tony Sighe, Change Manager at a leading UK Building Society, sought to address. After being certified to deliver the Tipping Point workshop, he used it to support change training to senior management across the business. In the following account, Tony describes his experience with the workshop and with measuring effectiveness at creating commitment to a change.

Leveraging the Tipping Ratio

I had been involved in delivering training on a rather dry change management methodology when I was invited to the Tipping Point certification training (to become a certified facilitator). I admit to being cautious at the outset, making the common mistake of thinking the simulator could be misleading. Before the training, I thought of the simulator as a predictive tool—totally missing the point that it was to get you thinking more about the interaction of the seven levers of change! Since that time, I've provided formal training to over 200 managers in a major building society in the UK. We have used the Tipping Point workshop across the building society, including the retail, head office, and subsidiary functions.

Use of the Tipping Point workshop concepts by trained managers creates a common language for change across the business. This has helped prepare management teams for transformation in their own areas. Templates for change planning now include the documented approach for proactive use of each lever and a forecast for expected outcomes. The holistic approach of the seven levers provides a tangible and easy to understand series of familiar contributing factors that together encourage and enable positive change.

After using the Tipping Point workshop in several change applications, we realized that measuring the level of advocacy at a point in time provides valuable insight, and supports the correct application of the levers of change. I developed a change analysis tool using a formal questionnaire of approximately 10 carefully worded questions that are used to measure:

- *If people understand the change, which is a measure of how effectively we're using Contacts, Mass Exposure, and Walk the Talk.*

- *If people support the change, which indicates the efficacy of how we're using Reward & Recognition, Infrastructure, Walk the Talk, and Hire Advocates.*

- *If people know how it impacts them personally, which reflects a combination of levers, especially Infrastructure, Walk the Talk, and Contacts.*

Each question comes with a series of statement answers to select, ranging from disagreement to full support, and each statement has a weighted score. From this a simple red/amber/green view can be assumed, with red suggesting resistance/apathy, amber suggesting incubators and green suggesting advocacy. The questionnaire does not capture or need individual names, but it does require job roles or grades, and the employee's department (from a drop down options list). Feedback comments are captured for each question and are crucial to help to explain the scores.

The results are simple to present and understand, and provide management with a clear summary. It was used to see how and where acceptance for the change was spreading and to inform managers where to focus their efforts across the separate roles and departments. Individual action plans are then created for each manager to further manage the advocacy in their areas. This encourages ownership of the change across the management team. It helps managers hone and target their efforts to Walk the Talk!

We continue to use the methodology and tools across many areas of the building society, and in my opinion we are moving toward a "tipping point" where the majority of the senior management will be trained and able to apply the seven levers in their transformation activity.

—Tony Sighe

The results of the survey that Tony and his colleagues developed painted a picture of the level of commitment for the change across the various departments in the company. It also indicated which levers were working for them and which they needed to revisit. Providing these insights helped managers Walk the Talk and improve their implementation.

Moving Forward

Key Concepts

🌒 The dynamics of the Tipping Point model result from recognizing that people's attitudes toward a change initiative evolve over time. At a given time, an individual falls into one of four categories depending on her attitude toward the change: 1) Advocates—people with experience, expertise, and enthusiasm toward the change; 2) Incubators—people who are trying to understand its effects; 3) Apathetics—people who have not heard of the change or feel disconnected from it; 4) Resisters—people who oppose the change, either overtly or covertly.

🌒 Leaders can foster change by using seven levers of change: 1) Contacts between Advocates and Apathetics; 2) Mass Exposure; 3) Hire Advocates; 4) Shift Resisters; 5) Infrastructure; 6) Walk the Talk; and 7) Reward & Recognition. Levers 1–4 directly affect people's attitudes and thus the flow between attitude pools, and are called People-Support levers. Levers 5–7 are called Environmental-Support levers, and they affect the context for the change. All the levers interact to help—or hinder—adoption of a change.

🌒 The tipping ratio (or ratio of new to Advocates to those leaving the Advocates pool) reminds us that it is as important to support existing Advocates as to bring new ones on board.

Points to Ponder

🌒 Can you avoid hiring just for your change? Are you in a position to leverage hiring for job skill, succession, or growth by ensuring that these hires are also Advocates of the change?

🌒 Do you have a plan for examining all seven levers of change for applicability to the change in your organization? Remember that examining for applicability leaves open the possibility of rejecting any levers that don't apply to your particular change or your organizational culture, but only after they are considered carefully.

🌙 Do you have a mechanism to see how many Advocates of your change you are getting and keeping?

🌙 Can you leverage informal networks to form an Advocates' community of practice, so that they can collaborate and learn from one another?

Chapter 4

Dynamics of the Tipping Point

When the effective leader is finished with his work,
the people say it happened naturally.
—Lao-tzu

There is no fixed prescription for change. For any given change, some levers are needed and others are not, but considering all the levers is essential. Using the Tipping Point model as a framework guarantees better decisions about using the levers. The chapter begins with a closer look at each of the levers and how they have been put to use differently in different change initiatives. The chapter contrasts the system-wide viewpoint provided by the Tipping Point with the linear view that dominates most mental and formal models of change, and it ends with two system archetypes that explain some of the important dynamics of change captured in the model.

Levers of Change in Action

> Give me a lever long enough and a fulcrum to place
> it on, and I can move the world.
> —Archimedes

Applying the Tipping Point model requires understanding the types of actions that exemplify each lever of change and how they interact. Some levers can be powerful, but also present a serious danger if overused. Others are useful in one situation and counterproductive in another. All the levers are more effective when used together. This section introduces these interactions. It begins by looking at the People-Support levers: Contacts between Advocates and Apathetics, Mass Exposure, Hire Advocates, and Shift Resisters, and ends with Environmental-Support levers: Infrastructure, Walk the Talk, and Reward & Recognition.

Contacts between Advocates and Apathetics

Advocates' firsthand experience with the change enables them to make a compelling case to their peers. Contacts between Advocates and Apathetics provide a vehicle for Advocates to explain their experience. They are also an opportunity for Apathetics to express concerns, which may require simple clarification or may uncover potential pitfalls in the implementation that need to be addressed. Contacts are essential to spreading acceptance of and commitment to any organizational change.

There may be some spontaneous contacts with Advocates and Apathetics, but there are ways to leverage Advocates and ensure more contacts. For example, town-hall meetings can provide a forum for Advocates, as long as they are not just information sessions. To be effective, town halls must be designed to encourage real dialogue. Participants must feel safe to air any issues they have, and management must be willing to let these concerns have an effect on the deployment of the change when appropriate.

Another good way to facilitate Contacts between Advocates and Apathetics is by identifying and using existing formal and informal networks and relationships between people and departments. (See more under Weisbord in Appendix 1: "More on Models of Change.") Informal networks provide a natural space for employees to discuss problems they have encountered and learn about appropriate ways to handle them. Working within these social networks can be a very powerful way to spread ideas, because the networks are made up of people who value and trust each other's opinions. Creative leadership finds ways to leverage the natural connections between Advocates and others and to foster further connections.

Finally, another way to cultivate Contacts with Apathetics is to make advocating the change a formal part of an Advocate's job responsibilities. But be careful not to overdo it. Taking focus away from other work can turn an Advocate from a trusted colleague into simply a cheerleader for the change. This undermines her credibility and effectiveness. For more on this, see "The Goldilocks Test" on page 131.

Contacts can be informal or formal, one-to-one or one-to-a-few, spontaneous or planned. Whatever their format, their strength is in providing a forum for two-way communication. Honest, reciprocal exchange, where each person is willing to learn from others, is essential to the effectiveness of each Contact.

Mass Exposure

In many (perhaps most) organizations, Mass Exposure is a very overworked lever of change. Every form of Mass Exposure has been used to promote a change, including posters, mugs, keychains, T-shirts, mass emails, broadcast voicemail messages, web pages, screen savers, and so on. Perhaps the most overused—or over-abused—form of Mass Exposure is the one-size-fits-all awareness training. This is not training that helps people learn the specifics of how their job will be performed under the change. Awareness training just gives everyone an overview of the change; this could include some straightforward facts about the change or the value it is designed to bring. Awareness training is in contrast to job-specific training that gives employees the skill and information they need to do their job under the new way of working. Job-specific training is an aspect of Infrastructure.

Organizational change implementers commonly confuse Mass Exposure with *communication*. Communication shares a Latin root with *common* and *community*. By definition, communication is participatory. It is two-way; it involves both sending and receiving information. Ideally, in communication both sides can learn from listening to each other. In contrast, Mass Exposure is typically one-way; information is imparted from those "who know" to passive listeners who are there just to soak it up. If there is time or a venue for questions, the answers tend to be superficial and a poor substitute for the give-and-take of real communication.

I worked with an organization that was devising a "communication" plan for the rollout of a risk assessment process. The entire plan was Mass Exposure, including glitzy screen savers, video monitors constantly playing outside the elevators, special newsletters, and T-shirts. There was not a single opportunity in this plan for the leaders to learn from the engineers who were to apply this process. There was no attempt to leverage the expertise of people familiar with it. The plan was implemented, despite my dissent. It was met with a collective yawn from the engineers who were expected to implement the new risk assessment process. This lack of enthusiasm resulted in a six- to nine-month delay in implementing the process, not to mention wasted money.

Mass Exposure has its place. If it is backed up with solid Environmental Support, it can be a cost-effective way to expose people to specific facts about a change. Relying on it to do more than convey facts and create awareness is ineffective at best and likely to result in more cynics than Advocates of the change.

Hyping a Change Initiative

Some years ago, a manufacturer with a large share in a regulated marketplace was instituting a customer-mandated quality program. The manufacturer had built its reputation on its ability to respond quickly to meet customers' needs. Its responsive reputation was being drowned out by quality problems with their product—visible to both customers and regulators. To continue to enjoy its market position, the manufacturer began a quality improvement program with a huge kickoff, inviting customers and employees.

The Mass Exposure program created real awareness of the quality program and the value that it could generate. Employees were interested in increasing quality, but few really knew what was expected of them. No new processes were put into place to improve quality. In the subsequent few weeks there was more Mass Exposure. Everywhere one looked, there were posters, T-shirts, mouse pads, and coffee mugs with the quality program logo. Hardly a week went by without a mass email extolling the value of quality. Employees were all required to attend a course on the general quality practices. Lunch-and-learn sessions featured professional speakers to inspire employees to value quality. Yet there was no supporting Infrastructure to gather and use metrics to improve quality. There were no rewards for improving quality. There was no training in the specifics of how to reduce defects and improve quality in their own jobs.

Before long, employees recognized that the media campaign was just happy talk because the manufacturer was not backing it up with strong Environmental Support. They lost interest. Over a year later, the quality program had hardly gotten off the ground. It was abandoned, and the manufacturer's market share was adversely impacted.

A systems engineer recounted a Mass Exposure experience that she had while implementing a six sigma quality program to improve product development processes. She was required to attend a three-day training program that she called a sheep dip because the ideas were presented in a way that was irrelevant to most people in the class. Very little of the course material could be applied to the everyday decisions that she made in her job. Notwithstanding, there were some Advocates among the students. These people were respected peers with similar responsibilities but in a different geographic location. They knew how to get work done at their company and understood and valued six sigma. Because of these Advocates, class participants had some useful conversations, sometimes in class but often during the breaks. She found these discussions constructive, and they gave her an appreciation of six sigma that she did not have before. Even more important, after the class was over, she found the Advocates to be excellent thought partners in helping her apply the analytic techniques from the course to her daily job responsibilities. In her words, "Mass Exposure leavened with Advocates can rise and even become a positive thing."

Shifting the Burden Applied to Mass Exposure

Some Mass Exposure is almost always necessary. It is tangible and can be planned, controlled, and implemented as a stand-alone project, making it easy to rely on it at the expense of levers that can be more effective. Worse yet, when the first media campaign doesn't work, or when its effect wears off after a few weeks, it is not unusual to follow it up with a larger one. The "shifting the burden" system archetype captures these dynamics of Mass Exposure. (See page 64 for more on system archetypes.) Shifting the burden depicts situations where greater and greater dependency is put on a symptomatic fix (such as Mass Exposure) at the expense of applying a more fundamental solution.

People often realize that the fundamental solution is more effective in the long term, but time pressure can drive them toward the symptomatic approach. The more the symptomatic solution is applied, the more resources are drawn away from the fundamental solution. The burden of addressing the problem shifts away from the fundamental toward the symptomatic approach.

Suppose you realize that many employees see an ongoing organizational change as the "program du jour"; if they ignore it, it will go away. A fundamental approach to address this skepticism would be to demonstrate value from the change as well as management's full support for it. This approach includes John Kotter's advice to create, measure, and report early wins (see Appendix 1: "More on Models of Change") and also includes rewarding those responsible for them. However, these actions take time. It is easy to be intimidated by the time investment needed for the fundamental approach. A huge media campaign, which makes people more aware of the change and could include information on why it is needed, appears to be quicker and easier.

A media campaign can positively affect employees' belief that the change will stick, but focusing on a media campaign draws attention and management support away from the on-the-job demonstrations of the value of the change. This leaves people wondering about the need for the change, which induces implementers to further turn up the heat on the media campaign. More focus on the media campaign draws even more resources and focus away from the on-the-job demonstration of value and management support. This is illustrated on the following page in "Shifting the Burden: The Danger of Mass Exposure."

Appreciating the pervasiveness of the shifting the burden archetype provides leverage to counteract this trap. If you see overdependence on Mass Exposure, it is time to break the cycle. It is time to emphasize producing early demonstrations of value and making sure all concerned have heard about them.

Hire Advocates

Sometimes it might be necessary to hire Advocates from outside the company to accomplish a change—especially if you completely lack the necessary expertise in-house. Nonetheless, hiring from the outside needs to be done very judiciously. If too many people are hired from the outside, resentment builds up against them. Everyone has heard complaints like, "They just don't understand our culture" or "No one ever listens to anyone from inside." By association, this resentment spreads to the change itself, making efforts to implement the change less effective and generally causing people to lose interest in the change and become Apathetic again.

The following narrative includes a creative way of recruiting Advocates while avoiding the pitfalls of hiring them from the outside. The Knowledge and Skills Framework (KSF) is part of a large modernization program within the UK National Health Service (NHS). KSF is designed to provide a more consistent and structured way to support learning and development of staff in the NHS. The goal is to ensure that the right staff mix is in place to care for the health, well-being, mental health, and social inclusion of people in the UK. Karen Dickinson was involved in developing and implementing KSF in the Sheffield Health and Social Care

Shifting the Burden: The Danger of Mass Exposure

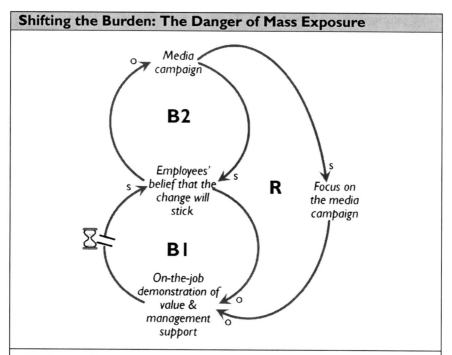

Shifting the Burden recognizes that a problem can be addressed in two ways, by a fundamental or a symptomatic approach. In the case of organizational change, the level of *Employees' belief that the change will stick* is the problem that needs to be addressed. Both a *Media campaign* (symptomatic approach shown in B2) and the *On-the-job demonstration of value & management support* (more fundamental approach shown in B1) will affect the employees' belief that the change will stick.

It takes time for the activities in *On-the job demonstration of value & management support* (B1) to be planned and implemented, indicated by the hourglass on B1. The *Media campaign* is quicker, so it is typical to start with it (B2). However, without demonstrating the value of the change (through the B1 loop), then the effect of the *Media campaign* will wear off. Worse yet, *Focus on the media campaign* draws resources away from *On-the job demonstration of value & management support*—further eroding *Employees' belief that the change will stick*. This, in turn, leads to further *Focus on the media campaign*, yielding a large reinforcing loop resulting in more and more dependence on the *Media campaign* (R).

(If you are not familiar with the notation of these link-and-loop diagrams see Appendix 2: "Notation of Links and Loops", starting on page 173.)

NHS Foundation Trust. The following is Karen's account of applying the lessons from the workshop and developing proactive, creative ways to gain more Advocates by going beyond Mass Exposure and cultivating extensive peer-to-peer Contacts.

Gaining Advocates for a Development Program

The Knowledge and Skills Framework (KSF) program began with a large media campaign to create awareness. The implementation plan depended on managers cascading the KSF ideas and implementing them in their teams. Two years into the program, an evaluation showed that nearly all job roles were included in the KSF outline, and most of the staff had been to training. However few staff members were actually using the KSF tools. Around the time of the evaluation I attended a Tipping Point workshop and recognized the value of the model in implementing KSF.

Initially, I followed the principles of the Tipping Point model in an informal way, using the main ideas as a guide and reference. I worked with people who showed the most commitment and enthusiasm and who were already Advocates (sometimes before their managers), and encouraged them to tell their success stories to others. These Advocates were in a position to influence the organization because they had the respect of their peer group. For example, hearing an experience directly from a nurse rather than reading a directive helped gain commitment from other nurses. After seeing how these Advocates were able to demonstrate the practical benefits of change and dispel the fears of those who were more skeptical, I began to apply the Tipping Point principles in a more methodical way.

The Mass Exposure campaign had created broad awareness of the KSF program, and there were pockets of Advocates. The challenge was to provide opportunities for these Advocates to work outside of the natural boundaries of their service or team. Apathetics seemed to be concentrated at first-line manager level where KSF was perceived as difficult and time consuming, and they could see little value to the change. This created a block in the middle of the organization and created barriers for front-line staff who were embracing the opportunity to evidence their work in a more systematic way and progress toward higher skilled work. Apathetics were not naturally exposed to Advocates so I began to look for ways to increase these opportunities.

One of the methods I employed was to manage training attendance by manipulating groups to ensure a mix of professions and services and also a mix of Advocates and Apathetics. I also used key Advocates to co-deliver sessions, participate in role play or simply as a "plant" in the group to articulate the positive benefits.

I made two recruitment decisions based on the principles in the Tipping Point workshop. Recognizing the pitfalls of hiring Advocates from outside did not alleviate the need for more people with knowledge and enthusiasm for KSF. I recruited two people on short-term posts who had worked in other parts of the NHS on KSF. Using short-term posts allowed me to build a legacy for the future using Tipping Point principles to build capacity (using Advocates) in teams.

Following the Mass Exposure campaign there were many Incubators in the organization. To give them the knowledge and experience to become Advocates, I invested more time in supporting two key groups—new and inexperienced reviewers and staff who had attended the health community programs. I established a mentor network among the new reviewers and specialist training, which had the dual objectives of increasing their skills and confidence and moving them from Incubators into positive Advocates for KSF. The other group was self-selected from the wider health community project who delivered KSF training to staff organized by job role, such as administrators or building and maintenance staff or support workers. The project aim was to create peer mentors amongst the front-line staff so that staff had access to information and support from their colleagues as well as managers. Another outcome of this project was to create practical resources and ideas for people to use in the development of a personal portfolio of evidence.

I found that the Tipping Point model helped me to understand some of the barriers to change and provided a way of sustaining my energy. It has helped me to view the process of change differently, to experiment with conditions, and to seek alternative ways of influencing parts of the organization. It has also given me a framework for negotiating resources and leadership from others. Mass Exposure launched KSF as a new phenomenon; using the Tipping Point levers of change has encouraged the right conditions for effective performance and development review. The ultimate aim is to create enough momentum for change so that KSF becomes fully integrated as part of everyday practice.

—Karen Dickinson

In the KSF program, Karen recognized the limitations to the Mass Exposure strategy that was in process. The Tipping Point model guided her decisions to set up constructive opportunities to leverage the experience of existing Advocates. It also helped her make recruitment decisions that encouraged Incubators to become Advocates and avoided the inherent pitfalls of the Hire Advocates lever described in the following section.

Fixes that Fail **Applied to Hire Advocates**

"Fixes that fail," another system archetype, describes the situation where a quick fix alleviates symptoms of a problem in the short term, but makes the problem worse in the long term. For example, using the Hire Advocates lever can bring in more Advocates in the short term, but actually reduces the number of Advocates in the long term. As illustrated in "Fixes that Fail: A Short-Term Fix that Worsens the Problem" on the following page, when Advocates are hired from the outside, it creates resentment. The more external Advocates are hired, the greater the resentment. This resentment reduces people's inclination to respond to Mass Exposure, making it less effective: fewer Apathetics become Incubators for a given level of Mass Exposure. At the same time, this resentment causes existing Incubators to be more likely to move back into Apathetics than forward to Advocates. The combined effect is that fewer Apathetics become Incubators and fewer Incubators move on to become Advocates, causing the total number of Advocates to decline over time.

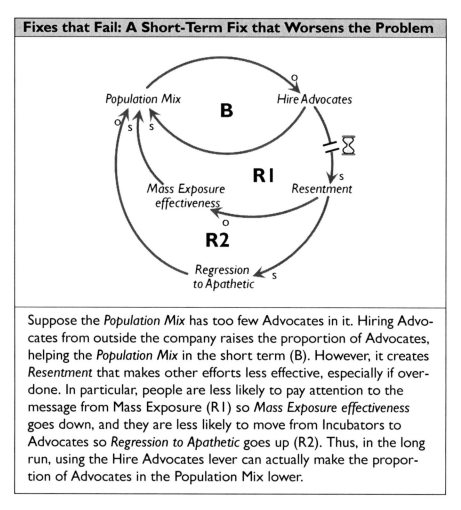

Fixes that Fail: A Short-Term Fix that Worsens the Problem

Suppose the *Population Mix* has too few Advocates in it. Hiring Advocates from outside the company raises the proportion of Advocates, helping the *Population Mix* in the short term (B). However, it creates *Resentment* that makes other efforts less effective, especially if overdone. In particular, people are less likely to pay attention to the message from Mass Exposure (R1) so *Mass Exposure effectiveness* goes down, and they are less likely to move from Incubators to Advocates so *Regression to Apathetic* goes up (R2). Thus, in the long run, using the Hire Advocates lever can actually make the proportion of Advocates in the Population Mix lower.

You apply a fix like Hire Advocates because you want results, but sometimes all you get is consequences. The lesson is to be very judicious about hiring from the outside. Be convinced that it is absolutely necessary. When you must do it, be careful not to hire any more Advocates that you need, and be sure that you also create opportunities for existing Advocates and even Incubators to help mitigate the negative side effects.

Shift Resisters

Resistance to change is probably inevitable, and it is tempting to believe that all resistance is bad. Daryl Conner (see Appendix 1: "More on Models of Change") distinguishes between covert and open resistance. Covert resistance is dangerous and can undermine a change initiative. In contrast, open resistance can be healthy and even make a change more successful. An organization that allows, or even encourages, its employees to openly discuss problems and issues that they have with a new initiative is less likely to drive resistance underground. More importantly, it opens the door to discovering potential glitches early in the process, before they become serious obstacles. How resistance is dealt with can have a greater effect on a change effort than the resistance itself.

If a Resister is in an influential position, it is important to know the source of his resistance. Addressing this concern may improve the change implementation. However, if this concern is not something that can or should be addressed, it might be necessary to move the person to a less influential position or to a position less affected by the change or perhaps even out of the company. With less influential people, waiting them out is often the best solution. As the change becomes more successful, their voices will be drowned out by the success. If it is necessary to Shift Resisters, timing is critical. This timing is explained in more detail in the section "Combinations Matter" starting on page 129.

Infrastructure

Infrastructure for a change initiative is often associated with equipment such as computers, hardware, software, and other tools. It also includes a well-defined rollout plan and tools and processes specific to the change and those needed to capture and disseminate lessons learned and measure progress. Job-specific training that teaches people how to use the tools and how to do their work under the new change is part of Infrastructure. A few examples give a sense of the range of Infrastructure that different organizational change initiatives require.

To implement a quality program in manufacturing, Infrastructure includes methods and measures for capturing variation, statistical programs for analyzing the variation, and possibly computers to run those statistical programs. For a supply chain management program, such as SAP, the obvious Infrastructure is software and workstations. Infrastructure would also include targeted training to teach people how to do their jobs under the supply chain management system. (This is different than one-size-fits-all aware- ness courses that are really Mass Exposure.) For an initiative to improve understanding of customer needs, Infrastructure could be the tools that market research teams and human factors teams need like prototyping equipment and survey instruments. It could also include aligning compensation or information systems to foster communication with customers. Last, implementing computer-based training for the sales team would likely require Infrastructure such as servers and courseware, because the sales team is typically on the road.

Of all the seven levers of change, Infrastructure is probably the most varied, because the specific Infrastructure required is tied to the needs of the change itself. Typically, Infrastructure is needed for every change, whether building a learning organization or implementing SAP. Adopting new processes, improving informa- tion flow, fostering new skills, improving communications with customers and suppliers, or building effective teams could all be aspects of Infrastructure.

Walk the Talk

Walk the Talk, or leading by example, is a vital Environmental-Support lever. Any change to an organization presents its leadership with opportunities to lead by example. These include making sure everyone understands the business reasons behind the change, clarifying the vision and expected end state, paying attention to results, and making course corrections as necessary, as well as ensuring that the other levers are being used appropriately. Walk the Talk is measured by the proportion of opportunities leaders have to lead by example that they actually take. Nothing speaks louder about management's resolve toward a change than seeing the sponsor of the change leading by example.

All too often organizational changes are seen as something that only applies to line employees, so leaders fail to see their own role in the change. They become skilled at "talking the walk," at using the buzzwords associated with the change, but not integrating it into their decisions and actions. Failure to lead by example signals a lack of commitment toward the change and always undermines it. For example, trying to lead a supply chain management (SCM) initiative but looking to the legacy system for familiar reports sends an unambiguous signal that the SCM initiative is unimportant to leadership. This undermines any prospect for success.

Linking the case for the change to the business's strategic plans is an important way to Walk the Talk. This ensures that all those affected understand the value of making the change successful and the consequences to the business of not doing so. This begins with having a clear vision of what the organization will be like after the change is implemented and continues by taking every opportunity to articulate the vision so that all stakeholders share it. Without a clear vision, a change is doomed; the everyday constraints that employees face will overwhelm a vaguely defined change initiative.

Once the vision is established, it remains important to evaluate progress toward the goal. This implies being close enough to operations to recognize small wins or make course corrections if necessary. Unless there is a clear vision and constant monitoring of progress, an organization is just flirting with a change and is unlikely to succeed. The following story illustrates a leadership team who started to Walk the Talk by explaining the problems of the status quo. However, they failed to recognize the importance of continued, consistent leadership.

Lacking a Clear Vision

A company with a diverse consumer product line had enjoyed substantial market share for many years. The firm was beginning to see its market share erode, and leadership feared that they had gotten out of touch with evolving consumer needs. They launched a program to understand and anticipate changes in their market. The leadership did an excellent job of creating a burning platform (that is, making the consequences of not changing so clear that no one could ignore them). As a result, everyone understood why the company needed to better recognize consumer needs in order to stay in front of new competition.

Realizing the importance of empowerment, the leaders drove the responsibility of implementation down to middle-level managers. However, they did not provide a clear vision of the end state or a framework of how managers were expected to get there. This resulted in turf battles among their market research, human factors, and sales teams. Each felt better equipped to recognize consumer needs and thus drive the effort. These turf battles put significant drag on the program. They moved the focus away from creating a better understanding of consumer needs to focusing on which team could dominate the others without challenging its own ideas on consumer needs. Had the end state been more clearly articulated by the leadership, or had they been closer to the action and better prepared for course corrections, these turf battles could have been avoided.

The company's leadership started out by making sure all they key players knew the problems of inaction. However, they did not build a clear, compelling vision of the end state, and they failed to monitor progress adequately enough to realize when the situation went awry, so they were in no position to make the necessary course corrections.

In *A Simpler Way*, Margaret Wheatley and Myron Kellner-Rogers advise leaders to adjust the way that they think about their responsibilities. They say that the heart of a leader's role is to create connections, provide information, make resources available, and let the organizing processes work. The leader must also establish the goal and motivate people toward it by making the end state very clear and establishing the dangers of maintaining the status quo. Their job is also to monitor progress, remove roadblocks, and ensure that the connections and resources are used. If progress is not what it should be, leaders should reexamine the clarity of the case for change among all stakeholders, and ensure that connections, information, and resources are available to all who need them.

In a *Sloan Management Review* article, Orlikowski and Hofman argue against a model for managing change in which the major steps are defined in advance and the organization follows those specified steps on a specified timeline. In the turbulent environment in which most companies find themselves, such a model is less useful than a more flexible model of change—especially when implementing technology that must be adapted and customized for an organization's needs on an ongoing basis. They argue for an *improvisational* model of change, which fosters experimentation, feedback, and readjustment along the way. An improvisational model does not mean trying to operate without a plan at all. Rather it allows the organization to take advantage of "evolving capabilities, emerging practices, and unanticipated outcomes." In fact, the authors argue that if you examine successful change

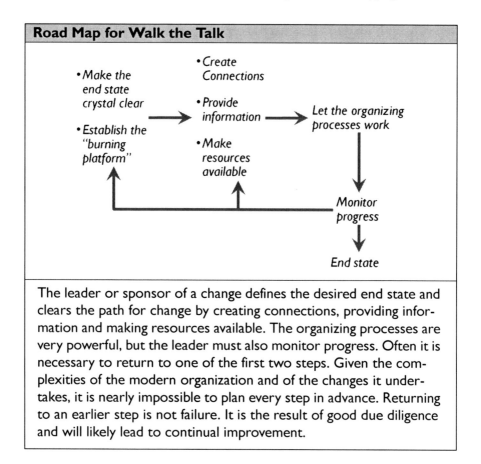

Road Map for Walk the Talk

- Make the end state crystal clear
- Establish the "burning platform"

- Create Connections
- Provide information
- Make resources available

Let the organizing processes work

Monitor progress

End state

The leader or sponsor of a change defines the desired end state and clears the path for change by creating connections, providing information and making resources available. The organizing processes are very powerful, but the leader must also monitor progress. Often it is necessary to return to one of the first two steps. Given the complexities of the modern organization and of the changes it undertakes, it is nearly impossible to plan every step in advance. Returning to an earlier step is not failure. It is the result of good due diligence and will likely lead to continual improvement.

leaders' actions carefully, they are already following the improvisational model, even if they see themselves as using a more traditional approach.

Reward & Recognition

Reward & Recognition represents the proportion of both reward and recognition that depends on implementing a change. Rewards are typically monetary rewards—salary increases, bonuses, stock options, and so on. Recognition can range from a simple "atta-boy" to a handwritten thank-you note to a formal award. A straightforward, sincere thank-you note can be a very valuable and cost-effective way to recognize an employee, and it can engender a strong sense of collaboration. Senior leaders who fail to use the power of their position to recognize a job well done are missing a huge opportunity.

Whatever form of Reward & Recognition is used, it is important to identify the key tasks to be accomplished to create the change and ensure timely Reward & Recognition for doing those tasks. The most effective rewards and recognition link desired decisions, actions, and behaviors to business results. Such incentives reinforce the business case behind the change and demonstrate a clear commitment to it. Look for behaviors and decisions that are required to make the change work. Then reward or recognize both the behaviors and decisions as well as the business results they produce.

Using the Levers of Change in Concert

None of the People-Support or Environmental-Support levers of change is a panacea by itself. The impact of each lever is shaped by its interaction with the others. All the levers need to be evaluated for their applicability to the change and the organization. The ones that are needed should be coordinated and used in concert. The following account provides an example of using the levers together to accomplish a change that was thrust on a firm by external circumstances.

Using the Levers Together

A large high-tech company had an organizational change imposed on it when two of its largest customers merged. The two customer companies had dramatically different reputations, corporate cultures, and approaches to business. The biggest change within the high-tech company was the effect on the two account teams who served these two customer companies. Each account team reflected the values and the processes of their respective accounts. No one, not even people in the customer companies, knew which corporate culture the merged company would reflect.

In the high-tech company, an account executive was appointed to create a new account team to serve the newly merged company. He had experience in both account teams and was respected by both. His new account team had to serve their customers during their transition and be ready to serve the merged company irrespective of which corporate culture was dominant after the merger was complete. He began by clearly spelling out the challenges ahead to both account teams. The new account executive commissioned a study of the strengths of each account team and their views about the company that they had not served pre-merger. Every salesperson's opinion was heard. Some salespeople recognized the importance of being ready for any eventuality in the merged company and thus were Advocates. Others maintained a bias for the culture of their own pre-merger client and felt that the status quo was good enough for the merged account team. The account executive made himself responsible to promote Contacts between these Advocates and Apathetics. He used Infrastructure to facilitate Contacts by creating an informal knowledge base to help the two teams get acquainted with each other and with their respective customers.

The executive was careful to structure financial rewards to support cooperation between the teams and to ensure the merged company's success. He dealt quickly with problems. He removed salespeople who were so entrenched in one culture that they unable to work with the merged account team. In terms of the Tipping Point levers, he typified Walk the Talk—sending a clear message that the change was important and why. There was some Mass Exposure, but it was limited to providing information. Contacts, Shift Resisters, Infrastructure, and Reward & Recognition were all used in concert. Hire Advocates was not needed. As a result, the high-tech company benefited from a productive relationship with the merged customer company for many years. By all traditional measures, such as sales, profits, and customer relations, the organizational change was successful.

The account executive realized the high stakes. He had enough organizational savvy to realize that no single lever of change was going to move his new account team into a position to successfully serve the newly merged company. His proactive approach—using six of the seven levers together—helped ensure success.

In summary, the People-Support and Environmental-Support levers combine to create the context for change. Depending on the change and the organization, there are several different ways that each of the levers can be implemented and combined. See "Reviewing the Levers of Change" on the following page.

Dynamics of Change

> You can observe a lot by watching.
> —Yogi Berra

The myriad interactions and feedback loops between the levers of change and the attitude pools make organizational change a challenge. Ignoring them accounts for the less than stellar success record of change initiatives. This section outlines some of the more important interactions and feedback loops. They are grouped into four families of interactions: 1) What goes around, comes around; 2) Combinations matter; 3) Not all levers are equal; and 4) The Goldilocks test.

What Goes Around, Comes Around

There are a number of self-reinforcing loops inherent in organizational change, and this section outlines two of them. The first depicts how the Population Mix reinforces itself, and the second

Reviewing the Levers of Change

The *People-Support levers* directly affect the flow from one attitude pool to another. Each lever affects just one flow.

Contacts between Advocates and Apathetics occur when people who have experienced the value of the change to their own jobs get a chance to talk about their experience with people who are Apathetic. Contacts affects the flow from Apathetics to Incubators.

Mass Exposure refers to one-size-fits-all training or a media campaign to get people aware of the change and provide a general exposure to the change and its value. Mass Exposure also affects the flow from Apathetics to Incubators.

Hire Advocates refers to bringing in people who would not otherwise be hired, but who have knowledge, experience, and enthusiasm for the change, and thus become part of the Advocates pool. Hire Advocates affects the flow from the outside into the Advocates pool.

It might be necessary to *Shift Resisters* to an area unaffected by the change, alter their assignments, or remove them from the company, but only after their concerns have been heard and addressed where appropriate. Shift Resisters affects the flow from the Resisters pool to outside the area affected by the change.[14]

The *Environmental-Support levers* affect the level of support in the environment for the change. They have an indirect effect on all flows.

Reward & Recognition includes financial incentives (such as raises and bonuses) as well formal and informal recognition (such as thank-you notes and awards) that depend on successfully implementing the change.

There is a wide range of *Infrastructure* such as job-specific training, tools to capture and disseminate lessons learned, or a well-defined deployment plan, as well as tools, software, or processes that are specific to the change itself.

Walk the Talk represents the proportion of time that management is leading by example, which includes making sure everyone understands the business reasons behind the change, clarifying the vision and expected end state, paying attention to results, and making course corrections as necessary.

describes how the Environmental-Support levers reinforce one another other.

Recall that the Population Mix is the ratio of Advocates to Apathetics, and is one of the factors in Environmental Support. When Environmental Support is high, more people will flow out of Apathetics into Incubators and from Incubators into Advocates; whereas if it is low, people flow out of Incubators and Advocates toward Apathetics. These flows determine the numbers of people in each attitude pool, which in turn affects the Population Mix. So, as the Population Mix favors Advocates, it increases the flow toward the Incubators and Advocates pools and away from the Apathetics pool. This will tend to drive the Population Mix further in favor of Advocates. The reverse is also true. If the Population Mix favors Apathetics then the flows toward Advocates will go down and those toward Apathetics (and Resisters) will go up. This will drive the Population Mix even further toward Apathetics. So the Population Mix ultimately reinforces itself. Stated simply, the more Advocates in the population, the easier it is to get even more Advocates, and the fewer Advocates, the harder it is to get more Advocates.

In another example of what goes around comes around, the Environmental-Support levers of change each reinforce one another. That is, each of them drive Environmental Support up independently, and all of them become more effective when the Environmental Support is higher. Investment in one leads to greater return on investment from all three. Consider implementing a customer relationship management (CRM) system. Every dollar invested in CRM Infrastructure is more effective when leaders Walk the Talk (for example, by using the reports from the CRM system in sales reviews) and when there is Reward & Recognition for employees using the CRM. Similarly, seeing leaders Walk the Talk makes the investment in Infrastructure and Reward & Recognition more effective.

The following example can help illustrate how the Environmental-Support levers are self-reinforcing. It is a story about a missed opportunity—about a company which could have been more effective by leveraging all the Environmental Support levers.

Trying to Make One Lever Do the Work of Three

A public health research firm wanted to expand the base of clients they serve. To help implement this change they gave substantial bonuses to employees who won research contracts in new areas, but they did not facilitate contract writing with supporting Infrastructure or leadership. They were not particularly successful at getting the new contracts they need to increase their client base.

The bonuses would have had greater effect if they were combined with Infrastructure and vice versa. The firm could have increased the Infrastructure support by targeting employees with proven ability to write winning contracts and supporting them with time to write, clerical staff, sending them to conferences, and so on. This would have encouraged employees to take the risk of writing proposals for contracts in new areas to earn the bonus money. If contract winners were rewarded by bonuses and other recognition, these employees would have become Advocates and encouraged others with the ability to write winning contracts. Had leaders Walked the Talk by clearly articulating the business case for contracts, this would have further increased the Environmental Support, making the Infrastructure and bonuses more effective. Together all three Environmental-Support levers could have been used to create the atmosphere to win the contracts and increase their client base, in a way that bonuses alone could not.

Combinations Matter

Most levers of change are more effective when used in combination with others. Some are even dangerous when used alone. Mass Exposure, Hire Advocates, and Shift Resisters are three levers that should never be used alone. Consider Mass Exposure. Some Mass

Exposure is necessary, but it can be easily overdone and create cynicism. When it is combined with high levels of Walk the Talk and Infrastructure and with appropriate Reward & Recognition, it is more effective and less likely to create cynicism. Similarly, hiring Advocates from outside the company can create the resentment that drives the fixes that fail archetype described on page 117. The likelihood of creating this resentment drops with better Environmental Support.

In another example of combinations matter, the effect of Shift Resisters depends on the proportion of Advocates and Apathetics in the Population Mix. If Advocates are in a minority while most people are apathetic to the change, then any effort to Shift Resisters to an area not affected by the change appears arbitrary or capricious—especially if the Resister is otherwise a good colleague and contributor. This can lower morale, which has a negative effect on Environmental Support. This negative effect can be mitigated somewhat by using the Environmental-Support levers. On the other hand, if the Population Mix leans toward Advocates, so most people recognize the value of the change, then moving a Resister out demonstrates seriousness about the change and sends a clear signal to the organization that the change is supported. This has a positive effect on Environmental Support, which can be reinforced by using the Environmental-Support levers.

Not All Levers of Change Are Equal

It is both tempting and dangerous to assume that if there are seven levers of change, then all are needed and all are equal. Some of the side effects inherent in Hire Advocates (see "Fixes that Fail: A Short-Term Fix that Worsens the Problem" on page 117) have been covered. The sensitivity (and its incumbent problems) of Shift Resisters to both the Population Mix and the Environmental-Support levers was also discussed ("What Goes Around, Comes

Around" starting on page 126). At the other end of the spectrum are levers without which nearly any change would be doomed.

Without Contacts between Advocates and Apathetics, acceptance of the change spreads much more slowly—if at all—through the organization. Personal contact can build trust and expose potential problems. Advocates' experience is essential to explaining what to expect from a change, and their credibility makes them references for it. Organizational cultures vary, and the form that Contacts takes will certainly vary, but Contacts is typically a must-have lever of change.

Walk the Talk and Infrastructure are also critical. Leaders who exemplify the change every opportunity they have—who build the new way of working into their daily practices—say volumes about how serious the company is about the change. Similarly, expecting people to implement a change without the tools, processes, and job-specific training puts undue burden on them and undermines the change.

The Goldilocks Test

Goldilocks, in the children's story, wanted the porridge that was not too hot and not too cold, the chair that was not too big and not too small, and the bed that was not too hard and not too soft. The Goldilocks test is finding just the right level—not too much and not too little for three levers: Contacts, Mass Exposure, and Reward & Recognition. The Goldilocks Test is not about limitations that are driven by budget and resource constraints and the need to balance the many competing needs of a company, including implementing a change. It is also not about the inherent risks that some levers carry if they are used at all (as outlined in the previous section "Not All Levers of Change Are Equal"). It is about the dangers of *over-* or *under-*using these three levers. These are levers that should not be avoided completely—especially Contacts—but too much of them can be detrimental.

Contacts are essential—they provide the mechanism needed to leverage exponential growth (see "The Power of Two" beginning on page 60). At the same time, there is a danger of burning out the Advocates or putting them in a position where they are repeatedly advocating to the same people or neglecting other work. The last one is especially dangerous. It undermines an Advocate's credibility as a colleague with valuable experience, and thus his effectiveness as Advocates is *seriously* diminished.

Similarly, some Mass Exposure is often necessary. It is a good way to get information to many people at once, but too much will almost always backfire, especially if it is not fully supported by the Environmental-Support levers. (See "Shifting the Burden Applied to Mass Exposure" on page 110). It is essential to match the Mass Exposure to the need for informing people on the change and no more. Never try to substitute Mass Exposure for real communication (see "Mass Exposure" on page 108). It is even more important to avoid hype; make no claims for a change that are not true.

Reward & Recognition is another lever where the Goldilocks test is useful—and surprisingly overlooked. While a substantial portion of Reward & Recognition must be reserved for implementing the change, too much becomes confusing or even threatening. On the individual level, a person who is hired as an accountant or engineer or salesperson wants and deserves to be compensated for the special skill that he brings to the job. At the organizational level, no company is in business solely to make organizational changes, so it only makes sense that the bulk of Reward & Recognition must be reserved for the product or service that the company is in business to provide.

Applying the Goldilocks test to these levers of change prevents wasted energy and expense that can become counterproductive. There is no formula that can be universally applied for how much is just right. The level at which any of these levers becomes too much will vary with each organization and each change. Keep Goldilocks in mind to prevent going overboard when ample resources are available or ignoring a lever when budget or other constraints are very tight.

Completing the Picture

The previous four families of interactions and feedback loops are all built into the Tipping Point simulation. This is a far cry from an image of independent variables each having an independent effect on the outcome. It is difficult to keep in mind all the possible inter-actions and their consequences and how they unfold over time. At least, it would be difficult for me to keep it all in my mind. This the value of a simulation; it allows you to experience the interactions, especially in a workshop setting where you can discuss the results and how you can apply them in your organization.

In the narrative on page 37 entitled "Tipping Point Concepts Applied to an IT-Enabled Program," Helen Nicol began recounting her story of applying lessons learned from the Tipping Point workshop at the UK National Health Service (NHS). After participating in a Tipping Point workshop at NHS, Helen saw the power of the ideas encapsulated in the model and the potential benefits of applying them to a major initiative with a large IT component. In the following, Helen concludes her description of her experience in building support for the workshop and how it helped her implement the change initiative.

⟨⟩ Tipping Point Concepts Applied to an IT-Enabled Program, Concluded

Change is complex, and being able to debate and discuss this complexity using the Tipping Point methodology and simulation tool has meant that more and more people are beginning to realize that they need to revisit and re-evaluate their assumptions, if the projects they are working so hard to complete have a real chance of leading to successful and long-term service improvement.

For example, the organization which oversees the IT program traditionally hired many consultants to support the implementation of the program and to advocate its worth within the National Health Service (NHS). This hiring of Advocates has, at times, led to tension between NHS and supplier staff and has often led to resistance to the change, particularly where Environmental Support elements are not in place, such as lack of senior management support (Walk the Talk) and little Infrastructure. The Tipping Point workshop helped people to understand the implications of this hiring and to re-consider it, and so improve the likelihood that change would be successfully adopted.

Workshop participants realized the potential pitfalls associated with the overuse of Mass Exposure and Hire Advocates. It led the participants to completely rethink their approach to communications and engagement activities. On completing the workshop, their original plan for a large, generic promotion of the change was radically altered and a more individual, people-based approach was adopted, including tailored training and road show events which facilitated a two-way discussion about the implications of the change. This enabled Resisters to air their views and led to one of the most skeptical people becoming the most avid supporter of the program.

The Tipping Point workshop has helped the team gain support and enthusiasm for the project. We intend to use the workshop as part of the development of new staff, when new teams form, to revisit projects in after-action reviews and to support project and program boards in their planning activities.

—Helen Nicol

Leveraging the Tipping Point methodology for one change helps create tools and skills that can be applied again and again. In Helen's example at the NHS, the Tipping Point provided a framework to discuss the complexities of change implementation. Through these discussions, they were able to expose and examine their assumptions. This process improves their ability to implement not only this IT-enabled change but future changes as well.

Moving Forward

Key Concepts

❧ There is no silver bullet. No single action that leaders can take guarantees successful change. Understanding how to put the seven levers into practice in your organization and how they interact is key to successful implementation.

❧ Some Mass Exposure is necessary, but it is probably the most overworked lever of change. Worse yet, overusing it typically has serious side effects that hinder acceptance of the change. Whenever Mass Exposure is used, it is important to balance it with strong Environmental Support and opportunities for Advocates to share their knowledge and experience with Apathetics.

❧ Remember the four key categories of interactions among the levers of change: 1) What goes around, comes around; 2) Combinations matter; 3) Not all levers of change are equal; and 4) The Goldilocks test.

Points to Ponder

❧ Are you constantly thinking about possible side effects, both short-term and long-term, from actions taken to implement a change without letting "analysis paralysis" slow your progress?

❧ Do you have a mechanism in place to monitor unexpected negative side effects from decisions? What about unexpected successes?

❧ Do you feel confident that all the key players are "on the same page"? Do they share a common mental model of the goal and how to get there?

Chapter 5

Applying the Tipping Point

It may be hard for an egg to turn into a bird: it would be a jolly
sight harder for it to learn to fly while remaining an egg.
—C. S. Lewis

An intellectual understanding of the dynamics of change is important, but experiencing these dynamics is critical. The Tipping Point model is captured in an engaging simulation. Using the simulation in a workshop setting helps managers experience the dynamics and interacting factors that affect the spread of organizational change. This chapter begins by outlining what to expect from the simulation and ends with a case study from a large high-tech company that successfully implemented a six sigma initiative. The case study demonstrates how the Tipping Point workshop provides an environment for a team to think out of the box and create an effective implementation strategy.

Getting Results from the Simulation

It's what you learn after you know it all that counts.
—John Wooden

Getting managers and change leaders together to play with the simulation in a friendly, workshop atmosphere creates a learning environment. The workshop gives a bird's eye view of the interactions unfolding over time, and provides the platform to ask "what-if" questions. Using a simulation with team members affords the opportunity to reflect on the organization as the team knows it. Too often people responsible for implementing organizational change rely on familiar techniques, despite limited success in the past. Using the simulation in an experiential and experimental learning environment helps teams improve their implementation strategies, and it's fun.

A computer simulation that sparks dialogue also accelerates learning. The learning cycle from a change effort is normally slow and often costly. From the start of a change effort to the end is typically a fair amount of time; sometimes a couple of years or more. The learning from a change can be applied the next time around, but this is just not good enough. Today's imperative is to learn faster. Tipping Point workshop participants apply what they know about change to the simulation and see and talk about the simulated output immediately. This dialogue increases their overall knowledge of organizational change and helps the participants think as a team. They can apply what they learn immediately—when it counts—not just to the next change effort.

The simulation adds an accelerated, low-risk, cost-effective engine of learning that leverages the knowledge of the team. Accelerated learning using simulations was explored in a master's thesis by Osamu Yamamura.[15] The following diagram "Increasing the Ability to Learn Quickly and as a Team" is adapted from his work.

Increasing the Ability to Learn Quickly and as a Team

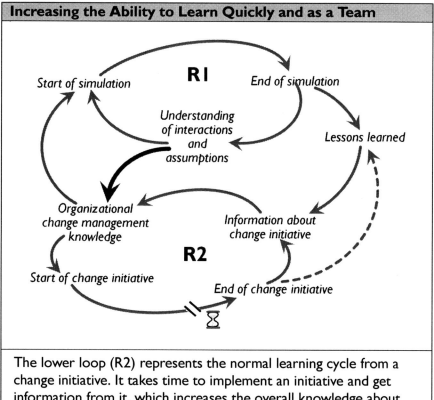

The lower loop (R2) represents the normal learning cycle from a change initiative. It takes time to implement an initiative and get information from it, which increases the overall knowledge about change. If there is a formal lessons learned (represented by the dotted line), it further adds information about the initiative. This increases our overall knowledge about change management—but it is too late to apply it to the current initiative.

The upper loop (R1) represents using a simulation such as the Tipping Point in a workshop setting. The workshop is structured to foster dialogue, learn from other participants and from the simulation, and bring out lessons learned immediately. This increases the overall knowledge of change managers, and makes it possible to apply these lessons right away to the current organizational change initiative, represented by the darker arrow connecting R1 and R2.

It is important to be clear about what to expect from the Tipping Point simulation. It is not a forecasting instrument. It is a powerful tool that can focus dialogue on change implementation. It helps teams see each other's assumptions about change, get new ideas, experiment, and see interactions that they had not considered before. Through this process, they learn from each other as well as from the simulation. They get a richer picture—a richer mental model—of the task at hand. This richer mental model is key to developing robust implementation plans that can make the organizational change both contagious and sustainable.

Dave Yarrow, of Comparison International, has been a certified Tipping Point Workshop facilitator for several years. He has lead workshops around the UK with a wide variety of groups and teams ranging from middle managers in manufacturing to local government employees and elected officials. He has worked with senior leadership teams facing the challenges of altering deeply ingrained cultures, and with experienced managers studying change and strategy in academia who are seeking ways of bridging gaps between theory and practice. He has seen the workshop work in all these environments. His firsthand experience with the Tipping Point workshop illustrates its ability to yield insights and increase learning. Below, he recounts some of his experience adapting and using the workshop with a large not-for-profit that needed to deliver a major change on time and cost-effectively.

Challenging Deeply Held Assumptions

Received wisdom can be a dangerous thing, especially relative to people's attitudes, behaviors and willingness to change. The Tipping Point workshop is an invitation to question received wisdom, to take time out to try some ideas and think differently for a few hours and then to apply the ideas to real change. The workshop is an excellent learning vehicle. It provides people with an opportunity to share their experiences of change and their knowledge and beliefs about what works and why. More than this, it provides a powerful tool that helps them to make sense of their experiences, and in many cases to gain insights that challenge assumptions that they and their colleagues have been making for years.

I worked with a large UK not-for-profit delivering workshops to help them apply Tipping Point model concepts to several important changes. The Tipping Point is a generic model, applicable to many changes in many different settings. However, if it is to fulfill its potential to help people and teams, it must feel accessible to them, and relevant to their context. The original workshop materials were developed around case studies from commercial organizations, with a focus on change initiatives typical of such settings. I worked with colleagues to develop case studies which illustrate similar points to the original cases in the workshop, but with situations that would be more familiar to participants from the not-for-profit organization. I also adjusted some of the language used in the materials that might be off-putting for workshop participants. (The language differences arise partly from the different circumstances of commercial organizations and not-for-profit public services and partly from transatlantic differences!)

After several years of leading Tipping Point Workshops, my belief in their value and impact has been reinforced many times. The real benefit comes when people who are working together on important changes can apply fresh insights to their plans and their practical implementations. They can achieve better success rates with their changes, and save time and money too! When they realize this, and do it, the real impact of the learning begins to show through.

—Dave Yarrow

Participating in a Tipping Point workshop demonstrates that the simulation works to focus dialogue and create a shared mental model of change implementation. There is also objective evidence. Michelle Shields investigated the Tipping Point's ability to stimulate learning as part of her dissertation work.[16] Her investigation used experimental field research conducted at a major airline.

Her goal was to measure both learning and team involvement using a case-study method versus using the Tipping Point simulation. On tasks designed to measure understanding of complexity, she found that the groups using the simulation did better. More important, she asked participants in her experiment if they felt that the team strategy reflected their personal input. She found that individuals who were in teams that used the simulation felt that they had more input to the final team strategy than did individuals in teams who used the case study. That is, using the Tipping Point helped move the team toward a common mental model of what is required to create change. Such a mental model goes a long way to creating the type of buy-in necessary to successfully implement a change strategy.

The Tipping Point's ability to create a shared mental model is also illustrated in the following account of a firm that implemented a market-focused product development process.

 ### Forming a Shared Mental Model Using the Tipping Point
A manufacturer found itself in a position where product decisions were made according to technical feasibility rather than market needs. As a result they were introducing some products for which there was little demand. To help them become more responsive to customers' expectations and to reduce their development costs, they introduced a new product development process. The process was designed to make product decisions based on market demands, to decrease the product development interval, and create value for the customer.

The implementation team used the Tipping Point workshop to help them focus their discussions around their project plans. As a result of discussing simulation results they gained a richer understanding of both the interactions captured by the simulation and each other's ideas about change implementation. As a team, they realized that they were relying too heavily on passive elements, especially Mass Exposure. They modified their plan to make leaders and key stakeholders accountable for active engagement around the elements of the new process. Years after implementing the new process, they reported how the simulation helped them "sing off the same song sheet" and improve their implementation plan.

Tipping Point Workshop Structure

The workshop draws on presentation, competition, and dialogue to create a structure that encourages learning and facilitates planning. First, the Tipping Point model is introduced with a real-world example to reinforce the concepts. Then teams attempt to devise strategies to improve on the results in the example. They apply their strategies to the simulation. Watching the results unfold produces a natural competition. The competition reinforces the model concepts, and it sparks dialogue to help team members understand each other's assumptions and experience about change implementation. The process is then repeated, going into more depth with the model theory and using more complex examples. This structure is illustrated in "Tipping Point Workshop Structure" on the following page.

The structure of the Tipping Point workshop is designed to enhance experiential learning while avoiding "gaming behavior" (attempting to beat the computer without considering the underlying concepts). Teams discuss, formulate, and document a strategy *before* they try it on the simulation. This encourages team interaction and dialogue and prevents people just trying out strategies without thinking about what they represent. In the short term, this helps teams form strategies that are richer and understood more completely by everyone. More importantly, they create a common view of change that draws from the experiences of the team members and from the Tipping Point model. They can then apply this synergistic, shared view to their own change initiative in their own organization.

Tipping Point Workshop Structure

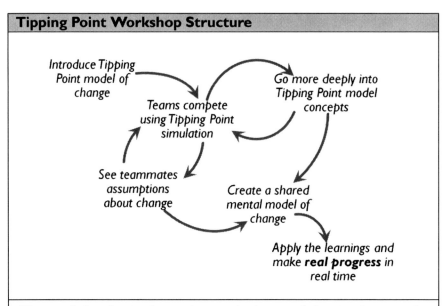

The workshop begins by explaining the basics of the simulation and the theory behind it. The emphasis here is on the attitude pools and levers of change and what they mean. A case study of a real change initiative (with lots of room for improvement) is presented. Participants break into teams and use strategy sheets to define their own team's plan for improving on the results in the case. All the teams' strategies are tried out on the simulation.

After the initial round of competition, more Tipping Point model theory is presented, followed by teams competing to improve on a second case study. Competition between teams reinforces the theory in the Tipping Point model and provides an opportunity to voice assumptions and to listen to others. Together, the new model of change and a better view of each other's knowledge help give teams a shared mental model of implementing change.

Finally, participants apply the learnings to a change that their organization is facing. First, they briefly glance backward to see how the Tipping Point could have improved a previous change implementation. Then, they brainstorm about the new concerns and opportunities with the current change using the Tipping Point model as a framework. Finally, they create action items for their current change from these concerns and opportunities.

Applying the Tipping Point: A Case Study

> The best parachute folders are those who jump.
> —Anonymous

Xerox Corporation was emerging from the most critical period in its history, one in which the threat of bankruptcy loomed. Having had success with Lean Six Sigma to stabilize the firm, Xerox was in a position to turn its attention toward growth. The product delivery teams were now being asked to deliver more products, more rapidly, and with fewer resources. A small, cross-organizational group was charged with determining whether the next phase in the Lean Six Sigma journey, "Design for Lean Six Sigma," would give the product delivery teams the methods, processes, and tools needed to meet these difficult objectives.

Heidi Grenek, of the Xerox Engineering Center, led the development of the Design for Lean Six Sigma (DfLSS) program electromechanical, software, and marketing content. Norm Fowler, president of Keys Six-Sigma, was a member of the Xerox corporate Lean Six Sigma Staff with the responsibility for developing and deploying DfLSS throughout the product development community. The following is their narrative of leveraging the Tipping Point workshop to embed DfLSS in the Xerox culture.[17]

 ### Applying the Tipping Point for Significant Cultural Change

As the team learned more about Design for Lean Six Sigma (DfLSS), it became apparent that much of what it called for had been tried and applied in the past at Xerox, but in many instances, the discipline and rigor had been lost over time except in diverse, isolated "pockets of excellence." We realized that if we wanted to maximize the return on our investment in DfLSS, then we needed to not only deliver the DfLSS program to the product development organizations, but we needed to do it in a way that

made the use of the methods and tools pervasive and sustainable over time.

Implementing a change initiative within a large corporation like Xerox amidst competing demands, limited funding, and a healthy dose of skepticism for "flavor of the month" programs is a challenge in its own right. Throw in the need to make it both pervasive across the entire product delivery community in three sites on two continents and sustainable over time and you have what many would consider a quixotic quest. After doing some research on models for change management, we converged on the Tipping Point model as the framework we would use to guide the development of our DfLSS program and aid our decision making. In a single one-day session, we used the Tipping Point workshop to familiarize the deployment team on the basic concepts of the model and had a focused brainstorm to prepare for potential failure modes and solutions for our specific initiative.

Through the experiential workshop and subsequent discussions we were able to better understand how to utilize the interdependency of the seven levers of change to drive toward the tipping point where DfLSS is embraced by an organization. Throughout our deployment we used the model to align our actions with our macro-objective of pervasive and sustainable change in the product development community. For example, early in the program's development, we focused on identifying existing DfLSS "pockets of excellence" within the development community. These were the individuals who were already using DfLSS principles. These pockets served as important home-grown DfLSS Advocates. It was counterintuitive, but we decided to train people in these "pockets of excellence"—the people who needed it least—first. By training them early in the deployment, we had well-versed, experienced Advocates who were passionate about their approach. They proved to be a great source of Xerox-specific examples of how the methods and tools could be applied, providing the examples that were integrated into the DfLSS training itself. By using Xerox-specific examples throughout the training, there was positive reinforcement that the methods and tools could be successfully applied to the sophisticated and complex products that Xerox was delivering. This hard evidence helped dispute a common myth that these tools could not be used in our products and helped make a better

connection to their own problem set for people who were strug-
gling to understand or embrace DfLSS.

These initial Advocates and their library of successful applica-
tions also enabled meaningful Contacts between Advocates and
Apathetics. For example, as the library of successes grew, we
started "lunch and learn" forums within each division in which
Apathetics and Incubators would get their lunch and eat it while
an Advocate was sharing a case study of how they applied DfLSS
methods and tools to solve a critical problem. The forums started
small, but as the word spread, more people began to attend to
find out about this new initiative. A second example of how this
library of DfLSS projects was used to encourage Advocate and
Apathetic interactions was the creation of a DfLSS track at our
annual internal modeling and simulation conference. DfLSS Advo-
cates were asked to present their projects to the Xerox design
community at large, which recognized their achievements across
organizations.

Consistent with the Tipping Point model, we limited our Mass
Exposure early in the deployment and restricted it to meaningful
examples of where DfLSS made a difference. We set up "virtual"
Contacts with Advocates via videotaped presentations and a series
of articles hosted on the Xerox intranet web site. These examples
helped identify Advocates to their peers and raise the overall
awareness of the program to the entire product delivery commu-
nity. A positive unintended consequence of this increased recogni-
tion was that it strengthened the Advocates' passion for the
methods and made them even more committed to share their
results with others.

In parallel to identifying practicing Advocates within the engi-
neering population, we also sought out and recognized managers
who Walked the Talk. These managers played a key role in the
overall deployment by not only supporting the DfLSS program
through the commitment of resources to training, but also by cre-
ating the positive work environment where the trained engineers
could safely practice their new skills. We recognized these man-
agers through a series of articles outlining their accomplishments
placed on the Xerox intranet site and in various internal and
external written publications. By showcasing managers exhibiting
role model behaviors, we provided examples of what others could

be doing with their own groups to support DfLSS. It also gave managers who Walked the Talk recognition for their leadership.

We also were fortunate enough to have managers who demonstrated their commitment to the program by participating with their engineers in the extensive DfLSS training. We had middle and upper managers who completed both the online training and sat through two weeks of instructor-led DfLSS Green Belt training. This not only gave them a deeper understanding of the methods and tools, but also communicated to the other attendees that the DfLSS initiative was important to their respective organizations. Even with all of their business priorities, over-committed calendars and other challenges, they found the time to actively participate in the training. Early on, we had a division president sit through the entire two weeks of DfLSS Green Belt training, with basically no interruptions from outside the classroom. This sent an incredibly important message through not only his organization, but the other product development related organizations as well. He backed up his words of how important DfLSS was to Xerox and the success of his division by carving out the time to fully participate in the classroom instruction, including the tests. That is senior leadership demonstrating Walk the Talk!

We expected the Infrastructure lever of change to be the biggest challenge. We had far less money and resources than we would have liked to do the "ideal" deployment. In hindsight, though, our limited resources actually helped us with our successful deployment. By having limited funding for classes, we were able to "cherry pick" the initial students and create demand for future classes since participation in the program was viewed as selective and a form of recognition in and of itself. By having limited funding for central program deployment head count, we had to partner with people in the business groups to implement our initiatives. This facilitated buy-in and was a good check and balance process for making sure we were delivering value to our partner organizations. By having limited funding for tools, we restricted the available tool set to inexpensive software that could be widely deployed affordably and was easy to learn. Not only did this accelerate the learning curve, but it encouraged people to use the tools and show others how to use them long after the in-class training was complete. No one became overwhelmed with having to learn a complicated program to do simple tasks. As their skills grew, so did their access to more powerful applications.

Lastly, our final application of the Tipping Point was in measuring our progress. As the DfLSS deployment team looked at metrics, we quickly concluded that the ultimate end measures of the DfLSS program's impact will be more efficient, effective and predictable product delivery. Given our relatively long product design cycle times and the time it was going to take to train, coach, and certify the entire product delivery community, though, we needed a series of in-process metrics that would ensure we were on track to meet our end measure results. After working through an extensive brainstorming, we identified metrics aligned with how we were doing on the seven levers of change as proxy measurements for progress with DfLSS. They were good predictors of whether we could expect the behaviors and decisions necessary to make DfLSS pervasive and sustainable across the product delivery organizations at Xerox.

—Norm Fowler, Heidi Grenek

At Xerox, Heidi and Norm adapted the seven levers of change to meet their organization's unique challenges. Initially, they limited their Mass Exposure to information about DfLSS. As DfLSS spread, they were able to transform their Mass Exposure and use it as a vehicle for their growing Advocate base to share their experience, while still maintaining the more personal contacts through "lunch and learn" and other mechanisms. They sought out managers who were leading by example, and were fortunate to have several to showcase. They leveraged their limited Infrastructure budget to help them create partnerships with business groups within Xerox and thereby increase buy-in. Heidi's and Norm's experience at Xerox demonstrates how the general concepts represented by the levers of change can be adapted to guide specific actions to implement change.

Preparing for Change

Experience is the name everyone gives to their mistakes.
—Oscar Wilde

In most organizations, managers are rewarded for action. Sometimes this leads to "shooting from the hip" with almost predictable side effects. It is usually worthwhile to take a step back and reevaluate the situation before jumping to action. A checklist can be a useful tool to help take the step back. Nonetheless, I offer the checklist in "A Checklist for Change" below with some hesitation. A checklist gives a very linear impression. It also makes all elements of the list appear equal. Never use the checklist alone—spend a few minutes reviewing the dynamics and the interactions inherent in change that are captured in the Tipping Point model.

When using the checklist, think first about the Advocates. What is being done to support them? What can be improved to 1) get new Advocates, 2) keep the existing Advocates, and 3) increase the capacity of the Advocates to spread the change? Remember that the levers are not equal, and they will interact to increase or possibly interfere with each other's effectiveness. Revisit the checklist from time to time to assess progress or modify plans.

A Checklist for Change

Contacts between Advocates and Apathetics

• Are the Advocates identified?

• Are the Advocates respected by their peers for their expertise in the product or service that the company produces?

• Can they apply the influencing skills described in "Skilled Advocates" on page 40?

• Can you foster Contacts through town-hall meetings or informal networks?

• Are Advocates being supported in implementing the change?

• Do you have structures in place for Advocates to communicate their experiences with the change?

Mass Exposure

- Does the Mass Exposure match the need? What might you be doing too much of—or too little of?
- Is the Mass Exposure always honest? Will it pass a no-hype test?
- Is the Mass Exposure matched to the support for and commitment to the change?
- Are you trying to use Mass Exposure as a substitute for real two-way communication?

Hire Advocates

- Is there a way to leverage hiring to include new Advocates when hiring for skill or growth?
- Are you in danger of relying too much on hiring new Advocates?
- Are you monitoring the resentment that often results from hiring Advocates?

Shift Resisters

- Are you surfacing and listening to the concerns of Resisters and making adjustments as appropriate?
- Are pockets of resistance identified?
- Do you have a plan to deal with Resisters?
- Is there resistance in key places?
- Are you confusing apathy with resistance?

Infrastructure

- Does the schedule match the work to be done? Do stakeholders understand the schedule?
- Do people understand how they will do their jobs once the change is implemented?
- Is there a plan for job-specific training in place?
- Are the tools, technology, processes, and other necessary Infrastructure in place?
- Is there harmful Infrastructure (e.g., policies) that must be removed?
- Are there tools in place to measure progress?

Walk the Talk

- Is it clear who the sponsor is?
- Does everyone involved understand the vision and the criteria for success?
- Is leadership making the business need/opportunity clear, and do all stakeholders recognize it?
- Are the decision makers and the decision-making process visible to those affected?
- Does every stakeholder see the link between company performance, the change initiative, and their own performance?
- Are all the company systems (i.e., compensation, operational reviews, business strategy) aligned with the change?

Reward & Recognition

- Are Reward & Recognition plans in place?
- Are you looking for the behaviors that make the change work and rewarding the business results from those behaviors?
- Are you leveraging recognition—including informal recognition?
- Is there a plan in place to reward or recognize early wins?

Interactions

- What areas need to be addressed simultaneously? Sequentially?
- What areas might undermine others? Enhance others?
- What other areas provide opportunities or concerns?
- What actions in your culture can make an idea contagious?
- Are you constantly looking for side effects of actions and decisions?

Moving Forward

Key Concepts

❧ Simulations are a low-risk, cost-effective way to accelerate learning—especially learning as a team. The Tipping Point simulation is *not* an answer machine. Every organization and every change is different. A simulation is a way to bring out interactions and feedback loops that might otherwise be missed.

❧ The Tipping Point simulation—especially when used in a workshop—has a proven ability to help teams focus their dialogue on implementing an organizational change.

❧ The checklist can mitigate shooting from the hip, especially when combined with clear recognition of the inherent interactions of the levers.

Points to Ponder

❧ Do you have a tool or process that encourages people to think out of the box with this change?

❧ Does everyone involved in this change understand all the factors and how they interact to create change?

Conclusion

It is not necessary to change. Survival is not mandatory.
—W. Edwards Deming

B usiness is done today in a world of change that is driven by political, economic, social, and technical factors that are constantly in motion. To succeed requires making internal organizational changes to adapt to and take advantage of this external flux. Many of us have been through many organizational change initiatives, and we have the T-shirts and logo mugs to prove it. Yet 50–85% of all organizational change initiatives fail, meaning that many needed, well-analyzed, and technically suitable initiatives never provide business value. The most important and appropriate initiatives is useless unless it is implemented so that employees can and do use it in their work. Change initiatives fail largely due to ignorance of how the change process works.

When leaders implement, or attempt to implement, a needed change, they have a number of choices. The Tipping Point model of change provides the framework to improve the choices leaders make when designing a strategy for implementing change. The model puts lessons from public health, systems thinking, and organizational theory together into a framework to create contagious and sustainable organizational change. It is centered on the concept that commitment to an organizational change spreads when people understand its value to their own jobs and demonstrate and advocate the change to others in the organization. If people are committed to a change they will work to achieve it. Leadership that fosters a supportive environment increases commitment and thereby the number of Advocates supporting a change.

Because the Tipping Point model has been implemented in a computer simulation, it enables management teams to gain "flight simulator" experience with it. Used in a workshop setting, the simulation can help team members surface and challenge their own assumptions and the beliefs that underlie their actions and decisions around implementing organizational change. The workshop encourages them to surface those assumptions in a low-risk environment, before jeopardizing business results by applying them to a real change strategy.

The Tipping Point workshop is a powerful tool for implementing change, because it highlights important and relevant issues that are missed in less systemic models of change. This improves the chances of finding areas of leverage in change implementation plans. In the words of Karen Dickinson, who used the workshop when implementing a career development program (see "Gaining Advocates for a Development Program" on page 114), "The Tipping Point workshop provided a practical tool for managing this change. Clearly it involved a lot of hard work; however, it offered a refreshing and pragmatic approach."

The friendly competition built into the Tipping Point workshop, in which teams try to outwit each other with a faster, cheaper, and more effective strategy in a safe, simulated environment, generates enthusiasm and thereby learning. The strongest learning feature is not from the outputs of the simulation—rather, it is from creating an open dialogue between team members. Playing in a simulated environment leads to experimentation and discussion that broadens understanding. Because it also compresses time, it shows the effect of the interactions in a few seconds rather than several months or years. This encourages experimentation that can lead to creative, effective implementation strategies.

The Tipping Point model is also an effective communication tool. It provides teams with a powerful common language to discuss and plan the change process. With a common language they can communicate clearly about the implementation and create a shared view of what it takes to succeed. It helps them align their expectations, and recognize—as a team—when they are on course.

Organizations change only when people in them change. This book is peppered with examples and cases of leveraging the Tipping Point workshop to implement change in organizations. The cases come from both the public and private sectors, and represent many different change initiatives and programs, including quality improvement, customer relationship management, career development, and others. A variety of industries including manufacturing, service, health care, and finance are also represented in the examples. The range of the examples demonstrates how the ideas in the Tipping Point model have been applied in a diverse array of situations to help people embrace new ideas and better ways of working.

Leaders are responsible for finding and instigating those actions that sway the organization away from the status quo and toward the changes that can have significant effects on their business. There is no panacea; every organization is different. A dynamic, systemic model like the Tipping Point makes the framework available to think through effective ways to push the system and instigate change. Everyone knows that reality is more complex than any model. But the distilled environment created by the Tipping Point simulation used in a workshop setting is an effective starting point to test the ideas and foster the dialogues that are prerequisites for successful change.

More on Models of Change

Statistician George Box once quipped, "Essentially, all models are wrong, but some are useful."[18] A useful model organizes the world that we experience. It simplifies and identifies the salient and important aspects of any phenomenon. Simplification, by its nature, hides detail. There are two types of models: mental and formal. Mental models are our internal representations of how the world works. People naturally create them to make meaning out of the diverse experiences in life. Formal models are theories that can be articulated mathematically or via language or in a computer simulation.

Both mental and formal models serve a similar purpose: to make sense of the world. Mental models are not public. No one can see mine or question them or improve them. Like most people, often I'm unaware of my own internal models although they drive my understanding of the world. In contrast, formal models are public. Anyone who understands the mathematics or language they are written in can both see and scrutinize a formal model. Thus a formal model is an effective way to share perceptions and even develop new ideas.

Models, whether they are mental or formal, result from integrating individual, distinct events into a cogent whole; they arise by abstracting the essence of many discrete events and then generalizing across them. Thus, models (mental or formal) are simplifications of phenomena that serve to create our images of how the world works. Since all models simplify, they are all inaccurate to some extent. The important question is whether or not they are useful—whether they help us improve and succeed.

There are two ways a formal model of organizational change can be useful. First, as an aid to understanding, it can provide a focused way to examine a change. A good model brings out the most important and relevant points. It helps guide the questions to ask—questions that improve the likelihood of finding areas of leverage and high impact. Second, as an aid to communication, it gives us a common language to discuss and plan the change process. With a common language, all the players responsible for implementing a change can communicate clearly about the implementation and what to expect from aspects of their implementation strategy—as well as what to expect from the change itself. Thus, by highlighting the most important points and by providing a common language, a formal model helps those responsible for implementation create a shared mental model of successful change.

The first five models that are outlined here are those of William Bridges, Daryl Conner, John Kotter, Kurt Lewin, Everett Rogers, and Marvin Weisbord. All of these models provide important insights for organizational change. They all influenced the Tipping

Using Formal Models	
Aid to understanding	*Aid to communication*
Highlight the important and relevant areas that need attention and energy.	Provide a common language that aids planning and decision making.

Point model of change. The last model is created by Patricia Zigarmi, Judd Hoekstra, and Ken Blanchard; it leverages the Tipping Point Workshop.

William Bridges

William Bridges's transitions model is concerned with how change affects individuals. It examines the psychological transitions that people go through when they are exposed to change and the pattern that these transitions follow. Because organizations change when people in them change, it is important to understand the pattern of psychological changes within individuals undergoing an organizational change. According to Bridges, there are three phases people go through as part of a significant change. The phases are: 1) the letting go or ending phase, in which people need time to grapple with losing something that has become familiar and safe; 2) the neutral zone, during which people need time to comprehend what the new order will be like once the change is implemented and how they can fit into it and be productive; and 3) the new beginning, where people begin to behave in the new ways that are required by the change. Bridges claims that one of the biggest challenges of leading change occurs because the leader knows about the change long before others in the organization. Therefore, she has spent time in the first two phases, at least, before the change is announced to most employees. Forgetting that they themselves took time to go through the phases, leaders see employees who are just beginning the letting go phase as rigid or even hostile to the change.

Bridges's Transitions Model

According to Bridges, people go through three psychological phases to make a transition: 1) letting go; 2) neutral; 3) new beginning. At any point in time people who are higher in management have had more time to learn about and deal with a change, so they are farther along on the psychological transitions path. Because it is hard for them to remember how it felt to be in a previous stage, leaders often see people in the earlier stages as hostile to the change when they are actually just in the stages of processing the change and how it will affect them.

Daryl Conner

Daryl Conner describes many of the important factors driving change implementation in organizations. Two aspects of his theory are important here. The first is the notion of participatory management, which means that all stakeholders' voices are heard. It is important not to confuse participatory management with evading responsibilities as managers. This is far from Conner's idea. Rather, he recognizes that people are more likely to support a change when their opinions have been heard and addressed.

A second important aspect of Conner's change theory concerns the roles that people play in implementing change. In his view, there are four important roles involved in change implementation: 1) Sponsors, who have the leadership role and identify the change that is needed and have the authority to mandate it; 2) Agents, who are responsible for planning and implementing the change; 3) Targets, who are the focus of the change effort and who are expected to make the change and to use the new process or new technology; and 4) Advocates, who believe the value and goals of the change but lack the authority to sanction it. According to

Conner, if there is no reporting relationship between the targets and the agents, then change initiatives usually fail. The archetypal example of this lack of reporting structure is targets who are line managers, but change agents who are in HR or another support function.

Conner's Four Roles in Implementing Change

Conner outlines "role axioms" for the four roles he describes:

Sponsors—Avoid overcommitment. Only sponsor projects that you are prepared to see through to the end. Without adequate sponsorship initiatives fail, costing the company and tarnishing the sponsor.

Agents—Avoid "bad business," when the sponsor has not sanctioned the change or lacks the resolve to see the change through. Never try to take on the role of the sponsor or attempt to compensate for inadequate sponsorship.

Targets—Seek clarity. Don't participate in a change unless you are clear what is expected of you or how committed the sponsor is.

Advocates—Don't confuse your enthusiasm for the change with proper sponsorship.

John Kotter

John Kotter emphasizes the role of leadership in creating important organizational change. He asserts that 85% of companies that he has studied fail to make needed transformations because managers do not recognize their roles in leading change. He recommends eight steps for leaders to follow to improve their success rate. In the eight steps, Kotter outlines the leader's responsibility to explain the need for the change, what the end state will look like, and who will guide the day-to-day efforts. He recognizes that the people affected by the change must be empowered, and that the leader's role is to remove obstacles. Kotter also emphasizes the importance of early successes in creating change.

Kotter Emphasizes Leadership's Role in Change

Kotter outlines eight steps that leaders must take to create successful change:

1. *Establish a Sense of Urgency*—Based on market and competitive
   realities, identify the problems of continuing with the status quo
   and the opportunities available from the change.

2. *Form a Powerful Guiding Coalition*—Form a team that works
   together and has enough power to guide the change effort and is
   committed to its success.

3. *Create a Vision*—Create a clear, well-articulated picture of where
   the organization is headed and strategies for getting there.

4. *Communicate the Vision*—Use every means available to communicate the vision and strategy, especially via the behaviors of the
   guiding coalition.

5. *Empower Others to Act on the Vision*—Look for obstacles to change,
   such as processes or structures, and remove them. Encourage
   risk taking.

6. *Plan for and Create Short-Term Wins*—Create credibility for the
   change by planning and demonstrating improvements. Recognize
   and reward employees involved in early wins.

7. *Consolidate Gains and Produce More Change*—Use the credibility
   from initial short-term wins to further the systems, processes,
   structures, policies, or employees who embody the vision.

8. *Institutionalize the New Approaches*—Draw out the connections
   between the change and the organization's success. Anchor the
   change in the corporate culture using rewards and succession.

Creating the environment for early wins, making sure that
everyone hears about them, and using them to institutionalize the
change, are key to a leader's role. There are leaders at every level
of the organization; these are people with a desire to learn and a
willingness to take risks. People look to their leadership. Effective
leaders lead by example. In Kotter's view, behavior that is inconsistent with the vision of the change will "overwhelm other forms
of communication."

Kurt Lewin

Many models of change, in fact many modern social theories, have their roots in the work of Kurt Lewin. His model of change, described in his 1951 book, *Field Theory in Social Science*, is often called unfreezing, moving, and refreezing. From his research in social psychology, he claims that an organization is constantly under the effect of opposing forces: forces of change and forces of the status quo. When these forces are roughly equal, the organization is in what Lewin terms a "quasi-stationary equilibrium." In his view, change is best accomplished by reducing the forces of the status quo, which he calls unfreezing the organization. He suggests "psychological disconfirmation" (or a clear, demonstrated discrepancy between the desired state and the current state) to facilitate unfreezing. In organizational change, unfreezing requires that all stakeholders must understand the challenges driving the change, why the current position is inadequate, what the end state will be, and the consequences of not making the change. The next step, moving, involves establishing the new behaviors and attitudes needed for its new challenges. The final step is refreezing, which is focused on establishing the necessary infrastructure to support the new status quo.

Kurt Lewin Saw Change as a Process
In Lewin's view, change is a three-step process: 1) Unfreezing—clearly establishing the case for change as well as an understanding that the current situation is inadequate; 2) Moving—establishing the norms and behaviors necessary to make the change successful; 3) Refreezing—establishing the infrastructure to do business in the changed environment.

Everett Rogers

Everett Rogers's now classic book, *Diffusion of Innovations,* reviews earlier studies of the spread of innovations within social systems in agriculture, health care, education, and other disciplines. The book explains Rogers's seminal theory of how innovations diffuse within a social system by spreading from the people most interested in the innovation to those progressively less interested. He finds that willingness to adopt an innovation is normally distributed. He divides the familiar bell-shaped curve into five categories: 1) innovators; 2) early adopters; 3) early majority; 4) late majority; and 5) laggards. There is an illustration showing the five catagories on the following page and a short description of them is in the section "Critical Mass" beginning on page 38.

Acceptance of an innovation by most early adopters can make the difference between a change or innovation spreading or not. Early adopters typically have more information about the innovation than the early majority, who depend on the experience of the early adopters to decide whether or not to adopt an innovation. Once the change is accepted by the early majority it has gained critical mass and starts to become to be a standard that is more easily accepted by the late majority.

Each person in the social system makes her own adoption decision by going through the following five-step process: 1) Knowledge is when the individual becomes aware of the innovation and gets some idea of its potential or how it functions; 2) Persuasion is the step of forming an attitude toward the innovation, which could be favorable or unfavorable; 3) Decision is about engaging in activities (trialing or evaluating others' experience) that lead to adopting or rejecting the innovation; 4) Implementation is when the person puts the innovation into practice; and 5) Confirmation is the opportunity for the person to evaluate results from the innovation.

Everett Rogers's Diffusion of Innovations Model

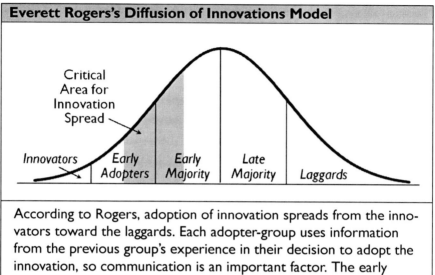

According to Rogers, adoption of innovation spreads from the innovators toward the laggards. Each adopter-group uses information from the previous group's experience in their decision to adopt the innovation, so communication is an important factor. The early adopter group often has many of the opinion leaders in it, since they tend to be well informed about the innovation and more judicious in their decision making than the innovators.

The innovation starts to become a new standard as the early majority adopt it, which paves the way for adoption by the late majority. This makes the transition from early adopters to early majority a critical area for the spread of an innovation.

Each step in the process is an opportunity to either adopt or reject the innovation.

Communication between the adopter groups facilitates the spread of an innovation because each group uses information from the earlier groups' experience with the innovation. According to Rogers, mass media channels are efficient for the knowledge step, that is, for disseminating basic information about the innovation. Interpersonal communication, especially involving face-to-face communication between peers, is needed to persuade people to form an positive attitude about an innovation.

Marvin Weisbord

Marvin Weisbord's six-box model provides a way to diagnose an organization's structure and how it functions and thereby work out how change can happen within it. The six boxes in his model are: 1) purpose or clarity about the goals of the organization; 2) structure, including infrastructure and systems, in place to achieve the goals; 3) relationships, which include relationships between departments and between people; 4) rewards, which include all incentives and punishments; 5) helpful mechanisms or the basic processes that any company must have to survive; and 6) leadership, which has the special role of monitoring all the boxes and maintaining the big picture of how they interact. In Weisbord's view, diagnosing these six interacting areas (visually represented as boxes) explains how the organization exists in its environment. He says that there are formal and informal systems at work in each of the boxes: formal systems prescribe how work should get done and informal systems describe how work really does get done. Any successful change agent must monitor the effects of the change on all of the boxes and their interactions, both formal and informal.

Marvin Weisbord's Six-Box Model

In Weisbord's model, six aspects of the organization interact via both formal and informal mechanisms. Leadership, as the central box, has the role of monitoring and coordinating the actions of the other five boxes, which are Purpose, Relationships, Helpful Mechanisms, Rewards, and Structure. Thus, Leadership is central to how organizations work and how effective change initiatives can be.

Zigarmi, Hoekstra, and Blanchard

Patricia Zigarmi, Judd Hoekstra, and Ken Blanchard of The Ken Blanchard Companies developed "Leading People through Change," which is a model of change based on two important goals: 1) proactively acknowledging and dealing with employees' concerns about change, and 2) involving employees in planning and influencing the change process. Leading People through Change is designed to help leaders surface and address the concerns of people impacted by a change by partnering with them to develop the business case, vision, and implementation plan for the change.

Leading People through Change is based on research demonstrating that people go through six predictable stages of concern during a change.[19] Identifying the stages and providing the right message and guidance at the right time increases buy-in and reduces resistance. (See "Zigarmi and Hoekstra—Stages of Concern and Strategies to Address Them" on the following page). Not surprisingly, the stages of concern that tend to come up early in the change process are *information* ("What is this change?"), *personal* ("How will it affect me?"), and *implementation* ("What do I need to do?"). Addressing these early concerns can produce and maintain significant momentum when implementing a change.

According to Zigarmi *et al.*, involving people in the planning process and making sure they have an influence on the change process increases their interest and commitment to the change and the effectiveness of its implementation. Zigarmi, Hoekstra, and Blanchard developed nine strategies for change leadership. Eight of the nine the strategies address specific concerns and have specific outcomes. The ninth, "Expand Involvement and Influence" is the central strategy, which underpins the other eight strategies and affects *all six* stages of concern. This strategy is fundamental to building buy-in. The table on the following page lists the six stages of concern, showing the strategy designed to address each specific concern with the corresponding outcome.

Zigarmi and Hoekstra—Stages of Concern and Strategies to Address Them		
Stages of Concern	Strategy to Address Concern	Outcome
1. *Information*: "What is this change?"	• Select and Align the Leadership Team • Explain the Business Case for Change	• Speaking in One Voice • Create a Compelling Case
2. *Personal*: "How will it affect me?"	• Envision the Future	• Inspiring Vision of the Future
3. *Implementation*: "What do I need to do?"	• Experiment to Ensure Alignment • Enable and Encourage	• Collaborative Effort • Infrastructure • New Skills and Commitment
4. *Impact*: "Is the change making a difference?"	• Execute and Endorse	• Accountability and Early Results
5. *Collaboration*: "Who else should be involved?"	• Embed and Extend	• Results that are Sustainable and Reach where they are needed
6. *Refinement*: "How can we make it better?"	• Explore Possibilities	• Options

There are clear connections between the seven levers of change in the Tipping Point model and the strategies in Leading People through Change. For example, the heart of Leading People through Change is Expand Involvement and Influence. Contacts with Advocates and others is key to Expand Involvement and

Influence. Some Mass Exposure can be used explain the business case and vision, but Contacts with Advocates are needed to create real buy-in and commitment. Select and Align the Leadership Team forges consistent Walk the Talk that is needed for leaders to speak with one voice to create a compelling case and an inspiring vision. Infrastructure supports the change and fosters Experimentation and Collaboration. Zigarmi and her co-authors use the Tipping Point simulation to help leaders understand the importance of the high-involvement strategies built into Leading People through Change.

Notation of Links and Loops

The language of links and loops is the language of systems thinking. With this language we can understand the structure of a system, and this structure drives the events and behaviors that we experience. An apocryphal story about a city family that moved to the country to farm helps illustrate just how structure drives behavior. A local farmer stops in to visit the new farmer and finds a scene of chaos. The cow's head is stuck between the boards of a fence. All the members of the city family are trying to shove her head back. The cow is bawling, and the kids are screaming. The local farmer picks up the bucket of oats from outside the pen and puts it inside the pen. The cow then twists her head and frees it from between the boards of the fence and munches the oats. The local farmer changed the structure and immediately the problem resolved itself.

The language of links and loops is simple and straightforward and can describe the structure of any system. Learning to read and write this language can be a powerful tool. First, consider the links. Simple arrows represent two components that are linked in a causal relationship—so an arrow from A to B indicates that A causes or drives B. The arrows are labeled with either an "s" for same or an "o" for opposite. An arrow from A to B labeled with an "s" means that A and B move in the same direction; that is, when A goes up, then B goes up and when A goes down, then B goes down. An "o" means A and B move in opposite directions—when A goes up, then B goes down, and when A goes down, then B goes up. A link with a cross-hatch and an hourglass indicates that a time delay is a serious consideration for the link. These labels are illustrated in "Link Labels" below.

Link Labels

Arrows in link-and-loop diagrams represent causal relationships. In both of the examples below A causes B. An link labeled with an "s" indicates that A and B move in the same direction. If the link is labeled with an "o," then A and B move in opposite directions.

When A goes up then B will go up, and when A goes down then B will go down.

When A goes up then B will go down, and when A goes down then B will go up.

A link with a cross-hatch and an hourglass next to it indicates that delay is a factor in that link. In this illustration, it takes time for A to have its effect on B.

The interactions in systems that are represented by these links hook up to form closed loops, which are known as feedback loops. There are only two types of feedback loops—balancing and reinforcing. They form the basic building blocks of systems thinking. Each type of loop has it own characteristic dynamics. These dynamics combine with each other to create more complex patterns. Balancing loops move the system into equilibrium or a steady state. Reinforcing loops drive the system away from a steady state, toward growth or decline.

In this book, the simple labels "B" or "R" are used to indicate if a loop is balancing or reinforcing, respectively. (Elsewhere, seesaw icons or negative signs are sometimes used for balancing loops, and snowballs going down hill or positive signs are used for reinforcing loops.) When a diagram has more than one balancing or reinforcing loop the loops are numbered B1, B2, and so on for balancing loops or R1, R2, and so on for reinforcing loops.

Considering the heating system in your home (mentioned briefly in Chapter 2) helps illustrate the language of links and loops. Working in combination, the thermostat and the furnace form a balancing loop. Together they keep the temperature in the house as close as possible to the thermostat setting. When the house temperature drops below the setting, the thermostat senses the gap and turns on the furnace. This raises the house temperature, thereby decreasing the gap between the thermostat setting and the house temperature. When the gap is zero (or very small in sophisticated thermostats), the thermostat turns off the furnace. Because it is colder outside, the house will begin to cool down. When the temperature drops below the thermostat setting the process starts all over again, illustrated by the diagram on the next page.

A House Heating System Is an Example of a Balancing Loop

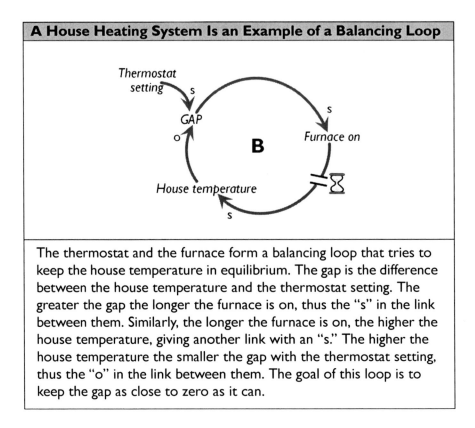

The thermostat and the furnace form a balancing loop that tries to keep the house temperature in equilibrium. The gap is the difference between the house temperature and the thermostat setting. The greater the gap the longer the furnace is on, thus the "s" in the link between them. Similarly, the longer the furnace is on, the higher the house temperature, giving another link with an "s." The higher the house temperature the smaller the gap with the thermostat setting, thus the "o" in the link between them. The goal of this loop is to keep the gap as close to zero as it can.

To complete the explanation of link and loop notation, let's take a closer look at a simple reinforcing loop mentioned briefly in Chapter 2: compound interest in a savings account. Interest accrued in each year depends on both the interest rate and the principal. The accrued interest each year is compounded (that is, added to the principal), which then increases the accrued interest for the next year (assuming, for simplicity, that the interest rate remains constant). Imagine that your great-great-great-great grandfather opened a savings account with £10 deposited at 2% interest before boarding the *Mayflower* for the New World in 1620. At the end of the first year, he would accrue £0.20 in interest, so the principal for the second year would be £10.20. The reinforcing loop below describes your great-great-great-great grandfather's savings account.

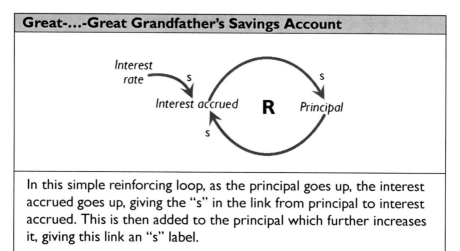

Great-...-Great Grandfather's Savings Account

In this simple reinforcing loop, as the principal goes up, the interest accrued goes up, giving the "s" in the link from principal to interest accrued. This is then added to the principal which further increases it, giving this link an "s" label.

The annual growth in the principal begins small: £10.20 the first year, £10.40 the second, and £10.61 the third year. However, if left to accrue interest for many years, principal reaches a tipping point and the annual growth suddenly becomes very large, getting larger each year. His account would be worth £22,598 in 2010. The same savings account would have been worth only £220 at the time of the American Revolution, £1,182 during the Civil War, and £6,620 after World War II. Relatively little interest accrued in the first 150 years, whereas well over half of it accrued in the last 50 years. Banks understand the tipping point, which is why they do not pay interest on accounts left dormant for too many years.

Growth of Great-...-Great Grandfather's Savings Account

The diagram above shows the principal growth on a hypothetical savings account with £10 deposited at 2% interest for nearly 400 years. The plot shows the characteristic slow growth before reaching a tipping point and rapid growth afterward. Now, if you could just find that passbook....

Endnotes

1. Throughout this book, "he" and "his" or "she" and "her" are used interchangeably to indicate persons who could be either male or female.

2. The anecdotes presented in the book are from personal experience and the experiences of my colleagues and clients, some of whom are cited and some of whom are anonymous. Many anecdotes are adapted to illustrate points made in the book. A few are composites of experiences in different organizations. My thanks to the many people who shared their experiences with me, both those who chose to be cited and those who did not.

3. See Yong and Wilkinson (TQM), Lancaster (BPR), Malbert, Soni, and Venkataramanan (ERP), or Rigby, Reichheld, and Schefter (CRM) in "Suggested Reading and Resources" on page 183.

4. See Jørgensen *et al.* in "Suggested Reading and Resources" on page 183.

5. This diagram describes part of the process of the flu spreading. It captures some of the movement between the three pools: well, incubating, and contagious. It is clear that there is more to the picture. This diagram mirrors many in the book. As the concepts of the Tipping Point model are built in the book the detail and completeness of the corresponding diagrams also increases.

6. Ryan, Bryce and Neal Gross, "The Diffusion of Hybrid Seed Corn in Two Iowa Communities," *Rural Sociology*. March, 1943.

7. See Tarde, Schelling, Gladwell, and Sterman in "Suggested Reading and Resources" on page 183.

8. See Strebel, Kotter, Lancaster, Vinson *et al.*, Jørgensen *et al.*, or Aiken and Keller in "Suggested Reading and Resources" on page 183 for estimates of the percentages of organizational changes that fail.

9. *The Fifth Discipline*, page 71. See "Suggested Reading and Resources" on page 183.

10. The equation for the number of grains of sand is given by:

$$\sum_{i=0}^{63} 2^i$$

This story is based on a classic folk tale that appears in many cultures. In the tale, a selfish king (or raj or emperor) is indebted to a poor woodcutter (or an elephant bather or servant). The king wants to give the minimum reward to the woodcutter. Underestimating how much he would owe, the king agrees to the woodcutter's "humble" idea to determine his reward by filling a chessboard starting with one grain of rice on the first square and doubling the grains of rice with each square. Long before all the squares on the chessboard are filled, the king realizes that value of the rice needed to fill the board is so high that he has lost his entire kingdom to the woodcutter, who also marries his daughter.

11. Internet growth statistics were compiled from the following Web pages: http://www.let.leidenuniv.nl/history/ivh/chap2.htm, www.isc.org/solutions/survey/history, and www.oreilly.com/gnn. All were last viewed January 28, 2009.

12. *Diffusion of Innovations*, 4th edition, page 209. See "Suggested Reading and Resources" on page 183.

13. Thanks to Sam Yamamura for this example.

14. In *Thriving Through Change*, Elaine Biech ("Suggested Reading and Resources" on page 183) introduces an acronym SHIFT Resistance. SHIFT stands for Surface, Honor, Identify, Find out, and Thank. Her recommendations are valuable steps that can be used to communicate with Resisters and understand their concerns. Do not confuse these steps with the Shift Resisters lever, which is about actually moving or removing people who persist in pushing back or disrupting change. Since leaders can get important information from the concerns of all employees, including Resisters, to improve change implementation, Biech's process can help bring out this information, and thus are important components of Walk the Talk.

15. Yamamura, Osamu. *Improving Quality of the Concurrent Software Development Management Using a System Dynamics Model.* Master's Thesis, North Carolina State University, Raleigh, NC, 1996.

16. Shields, M. J. *An Experimental Investigation Comparing the Effectiveness of Two Methods of Group Model Building Under Two Levels of Facilitation on Mental Model Development and Group Dynamics.* UMI Dissertation Services. Ann Arbor, Michigan, 2002.

17. See Fowler, N. E., *Lessons Learned from an Unconventional Design for Lean Six Sigma Deployment*, Morrisville, NC: Lulu Press, 2008 for a more extensive description of the DfLSS deployment at Xerox available at http://stores.lulu.com/normfowler.

18. See Box, George E. P. and Norman R. Draper. *Empirical Model-Building and Response Surfaces*, New York: Wiley, 1987.

19. See Hall, Gene E. and Susan Loucks, "Teacher Concerns as a Basis for Facilitating and Personalizing Staff Development," Lieberman and Miller, eds. *Staff Development: New Demands, New Realities, New Perspectives* New York: Teachers College Press, 1978.

Suggested Reading and Resources

Ackoff, Russell L. *Ackoff's Best.* New York: John Wiley & Sons, 1999.

Aiken, Carolyn and Scott Keller, "The Irrational Side of Change Management," *McKinsey Quarterly* April 2009, http://www.mckinseyquarterly.com.

Ball, Phillip. *Critical Mass: How One Thing Leads to Another.* New York: Farrar, Straus and Giroux, 2006.

Biech, Elaine. *Thriving Through Change.* Alexandria, VA: ASTD Press, 2007.

Blanchard, Ken, *et al. Leading at a Higher Level.* Upper Saddle River, NJ: Prentice Hall, 2007.

Bridges, William. *Managing Transitions: Making the Most of Change.* Cambridge, MA: Perseus Publishing, 1992.

Cameron, Esther and Mike Green. *Making Sense of Change Management.* Philadelphia: Kogan Page, 2004.

Conner, Daryl R. *Managing at the Speed of Change.* New York: Vallard Books, 1991.

Gladwell, Malcolm. *The Tipping Point: How Little Things Can Make a Big Difference.* Boston: Little, Brown, 2000.

Heil, Gary, Warren Bennis and Deborah C. Stevens. *Douglas McGregor, Revisited.* New York: Wiley, 2000.

Hirschhorn, Larry. "Campaigning for Change." *Harvard Business Review,* July 2002.

Jørgensen, Hans Henrik, Lawrence Owen, Andreas Neus, "Making Change Work," http://www-935.ibm.com/services/us/gbs/bus/html/gbs-making-change-work.html, 2008.

Kelly, Kevin. *New Rules for the New Economy.* New York: Penguin Books, 1998.

Kim, Chan and Renee Mauborgne. "Fair Process: Managing in the Knowledge Economy." *Harvard Business Review,* July–August 1997.

Kim, Daniel H., *Systems Thinking Tools: A User's Reference Guide.* Cambridge: Pegasus Communication. http://www.pegasuscom.com.

Kotter, John P. *Leading Change.* Boston: Harvard Business School Press, 1997.

Kouzes, James and Barry Z. Posner. *The Leadership Challenge.* 4th ed. San Francisco: Jossey-Bass, 2007.

Lancaster, Hal. "Reengineering Authors Reconsider Reengineering." *Wall Street Journal,* January 17, 1995.

Lewin, Kurt, *Resolving Social Conflicts: And Field Theory in Social Science,* American Psychological Association, 1991 (reprint).

Lorenz, Carol and Andrea Shapiro. "Infectious Spread of Change at Nortel Networks." *Systems Thinker,* 2000. www.thesystemsthinker.com.

Malbert, Vincent, Ashok Soni and M. A. Venkataramanan. "Enterprise Resource Planning: Common Myths versus Evolving Reality." *Business Horizons,* May–June 2001.

McGregor, Douglas. *The Human Side of Enterprise.* New York: McGraw-Hill, 1960.

Meadows, Donella. "Dancing with Systems." *Systems Thinker,* March 2002. http://www.thesystemsthinker.com.

Meyer, Chris. "Keeping Pace with the Accelerating Enterprise." *CIO Insight,* November 2002. http://www.cioinsight.com/article2/0,3959,675333,00.asp.

Moore, Geoffrey. *Crossing the Chasm.* New York: HarperBusiness, 1991.

Musselwhite, Chris and Randell Jones. *Dangerous Opportunity.* Bloomington, IN: Xlibris Corporation, 2004.

Orlikowski, Wanda J. and J. Debra Hofman. "An Improvisational Model of Change Management: The Case of Groupware Technologies." *Sloan Management Review,* Winter 1997.

Rigby, Darrell K., Frederick F. Reichheld and Phil Schefter. "Avoid the Four Perils of CRM." *Harvard Business Review,* February 2002.

Rogers, Everett. *Diffusion of Innovations,* 4th ed. New York: Free Press, 1995.

Schelling, Thomas C. "Thermostats, Lemons, and Other Families of Models." In *Micromotives and Macrobehavior,* New York: Norton, 1978.

Senge, Peter. *The Fifth Discipline.* New York: Currency Doubleday, 1990.

Senge, Peter, Richard Ross, Art Kleiner, Charlotte Roberts, and Bryan Smith. *The Fifth Discipline Fieldbook: Strategies and Tools for Building a Learning Organization.* New York: Currency Doubleday, 1994.

Shapiro, Andrea. *Applying the Tipping Point to Organizational Change: A Simulation.* Strategy Perspective, 1998. http://www.4-perspective.com.

Shapiro, Andrea. "Infectious Commitment." In Senge, Peter, *et al, The Dance of Change*, New York: Currency Doubleday, 1999.

Shapiro, Andrea. "The People Side of Change." *Leverage,* November 1998. Cambridge: Pegasus Communication. http://www.pegasuscom.com.

Sirota, David, Louis A. Mischkind, and Michael Irwin Meltzer."Stop Demotivating Your Employees!" *Harvard Management Update,* January 2006.

Sterman, John D. "System Dynamics Modeling: Tools for Learning in a Complex World." *California Management Review,* Summer 2001.

Strebel, Paul. "Why Do Employees Resist Change?" *Harvard Business Review,* May–June 1996.

Tarde, Gabriel. *The Laws of Imitation* (E. C. Parsons, Trans.). New York: Holt, 1903.

Vinson, Marc, Caroline Pung, and Javier Muñiz Gonzáles-Blanch, "Organizing for Successful Change Management: A McKinsey Global Survey." *McKinsey Quarterly,* June 2006, http://www.mckinseyquarterly.com.

Weisbord, Marvin Ross. *Organizational Diagnosis: A Workbook of Theory and Practice.* Reading, MA: Addison-Wesley, 1978.

Wheatley, Margaret and Myron Kellner-Rogers. *A Simpler Way.* San Francisco: Berrett-Koehler Publishers, 1996.

Yong, Josephine and Adrian Wilkinson. "Rethinking Total Quality Management." *Total Quality Management,* 2001, 247–258.

Acknowledgments

A second edition, by its nature, builds on the first, and I am grateful to those whose support contributed to the first edition. This edition would never have been possible without the advocacy and contribution of clients and colleagues. Many have contributed their experiences to this book, both anonymously and with attribution. Besides their direct contributions to this book, I have learned immeasurably from working with them.

I also owe a debt to Peter Anlyan, Mara Evans, and Maria Tadd who read and commented on earlier drafts of this edition. Thanks to Annette Shaked who suggested a rename of one of the levers of change, and to Al Toews, Dave Yarrow, and Pat Zigarmi who helped me think through the consequences of the change. As with the first edition, Jennie Ratcliffe contributed greatly by patiently helping me work through ideas and make them clear. Finally, my thanks to Ted Ruybal for the cover design, Karen Newton for the interior page layout, and Laura Poole for editing.

Acknowledgments to the First Edition

Without the support and advice of many people this book would never have been possible. Let me first thank the clients and colleagues that I have worked with and learned from over the years. I also wish to thank Roger Bushnell, Kimm Hershberger, Art

Kleiner, Rick Ross, Michelle Shields, Judy Seidenstein, Janet Smith, Sue Tideman, and Carol Willett who read and commented on earlier drafts of the book. It has been strengthened to the extent that I heeded their comments, and any oversights are my own.

Special thanks to Carol Lorenz who encouraged me to pursue System Dynamics Modeling and thus made the simulation a possibility. Sam Yamamura taught me the Japanese proverb that brilliantly illustrates the power of systems thinking. Conversations with George Smart helped me frame the position the book would occupy. I also owe a special debt to Pat Carstensen and Jennie Ratcliffe, whose unflinching willingness to hear and hone my latest idea contributed greatly to the intellectual backbone of the book. Finally my editor, Laura Poole, made my prose readable and Susan Bilheimer guided me through the production process.

Notes on Contributors

A special thanks to the following people who contributed their experience applying lessons from the Tipping Point workshop in their organizations. Their experiences deeply enrich this book. I also own a debt of gratitude to others who contributed their stories anonymously.

Karen Dickinson is Learning and Development Manager for Sheffield Health and Social Care UK National Health Service (NHS) Foundation Trust. She manages the learning and development designing and commissioning training to meet organizational needs, with particular emphasis on the development of our support staff. She oversees the integration of the NHS Knowledge and Skills Framework; promotes effective performance review systems; and supports learning and development in the workplace through vocational qualifications. Karen can be reached via email at Karen.Dickinson@shsc.nhs.uk.

Norm Fowler was a member of the Xerox corporate Lean Six Sigma Staff with the responsibility of developing and deploying Design for Lean Six Sigma throughout the product development community. Norm currently is President of Keys Six Sigma (http://www.keys6sigma.com), a consulting company established to help all size companies sort through the issues and concerns about developing and deploying a Lean Six Sigma programs. He can be reached by email at normfowler@keys6sigma.com.

Heidi Grenek was a member of the Xerox Engineering Center, leading the development of the Design for Lean Six Sigma program electro-mechanical, software, and marketing content. Her focus was on using systems thinking to create a program in which the DfLSS methods, processes, and tools became both pervasive and sustainable across Xerox. Heidi has subsequently moved on to other program leadership roles at Xerox. Heidi can be reached at Heidi.Grenek@xerox.com.

Helen Nicol is a organizational development professional specializing in learning and knowledge sharing. Currently a civil servant with the UK Department for Work and Pensions. Helen has a keen interest in people's reaction to and motivation for change. A bit of a techie, she enjoys online interaction and can be contacted through her blog—The Business of Knowing http://thebusinessof-knowing.blogspot.com/, or at Twitter @helennicol.

Warren Scott is a gestalt trained organizational consultant. Warren's consultancy, Oakwood Learning (http://www.oakwoodlearning.com) works predominantly with organizations in relation to the human aspects of change. He helps organizations going through change to create advocates, and to ensure that the advocates have the skills to be influential in making the business successful. Warren can be reached via e-mail at warren@oakwoodlearning.com.

Dan Siems is a finance-focused operations executive and can be found at http://www.OperatingCurve.com. Dan specializes in translating strategy into action by blending factory physics, theory of constraints, management measurement systems, and change management to bring about fast, sustainable, and lasting improvement. Dan's email address is dan.siems@OperatingCurve.com.

Tony Sighe has over 20 years of change-related experience in a career spanning operations management, business consultancy, and corporate project management. He has held roles as Change Manager on large retail and IT transformation programs. Tony has delivered the Tipping Point workshop to several hundred managers. He developed tangible survey and analysis tools to measure progress, commitment, and success of change, linked to the Tipping Point model principles. Contact Tony by email at tsighe@aol.com or see http://www.tippingpointchange.com.

Dave Yarrow has been practicing, teaching, and researching business excellence and organizational change for 25 years. He is Development Manager on the global best practice benchmarking program, managed by Comparison International Limited, http://www.comparisonintl.com. Dave is an Associate Fellow at Warwick Business School and an External Member of Teesside University's Centre for Leadership and Organizational Change. Dave has been leading Tipping Point Workshops regularly since 2004, and during 2008 qualified as a Master Trainer, authorized to train and accredit others as Workshop Facilitators. Dave can be reached via email at davidy@comparisonintl.com.

Patricia Zigarmi is a founder of The Ken Blanchard Companies. Pat is an expert in the areas of leadership and change management and is coauthor of *Leading at a Higher Level: Blanchard on Leadership* and *Creating High Performing Organizations,* and *Leadership and the One Minute Manager.* She has been a business coach and advisor to many executives and has coauthored many Blanchard training programs and products, including Situational Leadership® II, and Leading People through Change. Pat's email address is pat.zigarmi@kenblanchard.com.

Index

About the Author

For over twenty-five years, Dr. Andrea Shapiro has worked with organizations to optimize their effectiveness through innovative learning methods and improved decision making. She brings a unique perspective to organizational change based on experience in software development, business modeling, management, and organizational learning and development.

Andrea designed and developed the Tipping Point computer simulation and workshop in 1997 after seeing so many well-meaning change efforts miss their mark. She has delivered the workshop to major corporations, non-profits, and government agencies in the United States, Canada, and Europe, and has accredited hundreds of change leaders and consultants to deliver the workshop worldwide. *Creating Contagious Commitment* gives detailed examples, theory, and background, all of which will appeal to any manager faced with implementing a significant organizational change. The second edition includes many additional real-life accounts from change leaders describing how they applied learnings from the Tipping Point workshop to a wide range of change initiatives in diverse organizations from high-tech companies to hospitals and banks.

After earning master's degrees in mathematics and psychology and a doctorate in behavioral decision making, Andrea went on to further studies at the Coaches Institute and the MIT Sloan Business School executive education program in system dynamics. She has also served on the Graduate Faculty at UNC Chapel Hill and taught decision making at Pfeiffer University's graduate program in organizational management.

For more information on a Tipping Point Workshop or
on training and certification please visit:
www.4-perspective.com

or email
ccc@4-perspective.com